To:

_____

From:

_____

Date:

_____

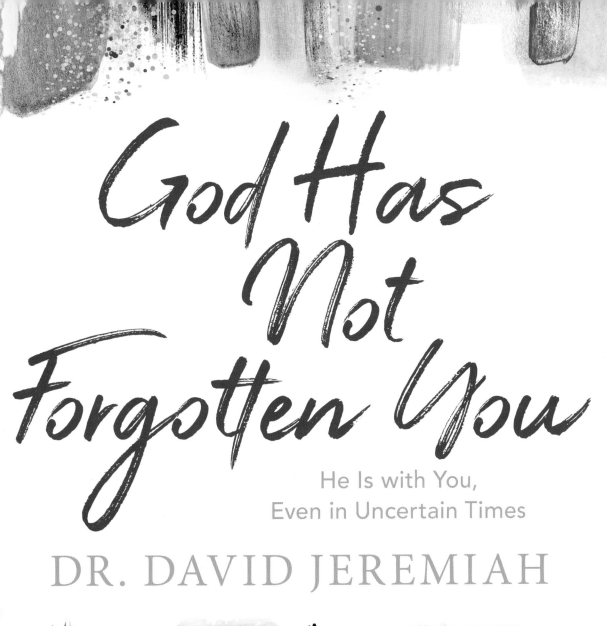

God Has Not Forgotten You

He Is with You, Even in Uncertain Times

DR. DAVID JEREMIAH

THOMAS NELSON
Since 1798

God Has Not Forgotten You

© 2021 David P. Jeremiah

Published in Nashville, Tennessee, by Thomas Nelson. Thomas Nelson is a registered trademark of HarperCollins Christian Publishing, Inc.

Published in association with Yates & Yates, www.yates2.com.

Thomas Nelson titles may be purchased in bulk for educational, business, fund-raising, or sales promotional use. For information, please e-mail SpecialMarkets@ ThomasNelson.com.

ISBN 978-1-4002-1136-4 (HC)
ISBN 978-1-4002-3039-6 (audiobook)
ISBN 978-1-4002-1137-1 (eBook)

Printed in India
21 22 23 24 25 REP 10 9 8 7 6 5 4 3 2 1

The LORD also will be a refuge for the oppressed, a refuge in times of trouble. And those who know Your name will put their trust in You; for You, LORD, have not forsaken those who seek You.

PSALM 9:9–10

CONTENTS

YOU ARE NOT ALONE

According to an old African proverb, "Smooth seas do not make skillful sailors." Oh, how we wish that were not the case!

As a people, we love smooth seas and sunny days. If we had our way, there would be no storms, no clouds, no sorrows, and no losses. Unfortunately, we don't have our way, which is why we are so often disappointed, discouraged, and distressed.

Just as bad, the "weather" in our lives changes quickly. Without warning we can encounter devastating circumstances—including the loss of our homes, of those dear to us, of money and possessions, of health, of employment, and even of our faith and hope.

The men and women profiled in the Bible understood this reality. Just ask Job! He was living his life with an abundance of blessings: a wonderful family, wealth to last for generations, and a deep and personal connection to Almighty God. Then, in the blink of an eye, it all came crashing down. You could also ask Hannah, who endured years of frustration and despair because her longing for a child was unfulfilled. Or ask Jeremiah, "the weeping prophet," who witnessed the destruction of Jerusalem and was so filled with grief that he wrote a book called Lamentations. Or ask Paul, who not only carried the burden of his past persecution of God's people but was also afflicted with all manner of attacks and attempts on his life throughout his ministry on behalf of the Gospel.

You could also ask Jesus, who—even before He was betrayed by His disciples and crucified on a Roman cross—offered this warning: "In the world you will have tribulation" (John 16:33).

I don't know the particulars of your life, but whatever your circumstance, I'm confident you understand these realities as well. We're living in a world that can change rapidly. One terrorist act, one natural disaster, one health pandemic, one economic collapse, one nuclear weapon—one example of any number of potential crises, and our lives will change overnight.

Our individual lives are just as fragile. The roof over our head may be gone tomorrow. The money in our savings account might disappear. Those dear to us in our immediate family circle may be absent in the near future. The fragility of life alone generates uncertainty and fear in some people.

Perhaps worst of all is the feeling of being abandoned in the midst of all this uncertainty. It's one thing to endure hardship as part of a group—to navigate difficult waters under the discerning gaze of a competent captain who is able to bring you through any storm and land you at a place of safety. It's entirely something else to endure that storm on your own. To feel as if no one else sees and no one else cares.

In short, difficult circumstances will always be difficult. But their effect is multiplied tenfold when we feel like God has forgotten us.

So, we need to look honestly at that question: Does God forget about us? Does He lose sight of us? Does He stop caring about the circumstances of our lives and what we are being forced to endure?

Let's answer that question by looking back at Jesus' warning in John 16:33: "In the world you will have tribulation." In my Bible, there isn't a period after the word *tribulation*. There's a semicolon: "In the world you will have tribulation; but be of good cheer, I have overcome the world."

Praise God for that semicolon! It tells us that all of our losses are temporary and all of our blessings are permanent. We need not cower in fear of the future or worry about the present. Instead, we have a heavenly Captain who has overcome the world and knows the way to lead us through any storm.

We need to look honestly at that question: Does God forget about us?

Because of who Jesus is and what He has done, here are just a few of the promises we can claim:

- In the power of Jesus Christ, we are more than conquerors (Romans 8:37).
- Nothing can separate us from His love (Romans 8:38–39).
- All things work together for good (Romans 8:28).
- Those who wait upon Him will renew their strength (Isaiah 40:31).
- We can do all things through Him who strengthens us (Philippians 4:13).
- We can even "count it all joy" when we face trials (James 1:2).
- And we can trust the One who said, "I will never leave you nor forsake you" (Hebrews 13:5).

In short, God has not forgotten us!

More specifically, He has not forgotten you. He is with you even during the most troublesome times and difficult days. He is with you even now.

Let's look again at John 16:33 and these words of Jesus: "These things I have spoken to you, that in Me you may have peace. In the world you will have tribulation; but be of good cheer, I have overcome the world." Before the word *tribulation* is *peace*, and after *tribulation* is the word *cheer*. Jesus Himself is the opening and closing: "I have spoken" and "I have overcome." And we are in Him!

J. I. Packer wrote the following in his book *Knowing God*:

> We should not, therefore, be too taken aback when unexpected and upsetting and discouraging things happen to us now. What do they mean? Simply that God in his wisdom means to make something of us which we have not attained yet, and he is dealing with us accordingly. . . .
>
> It is often the case, as all the saints know, that fellowship with the Father and the Son is most vivid and sweet, and Christian joy is the greatest, when the cross is heaviest.[1]

Packer then suggested two ways of handling the trials of life when we cannot, for the moment, see God's purpose in them. "First, by taking them as from God, and asking ourselves what reactions to them, and in them, the gospel of God requires of us; second, by seeking God's face specifically about them. If we do these two things, we shall never find ourselves wholly in the dark as to God's purpose in our troubles."[2]

I've written this book to help you do those things in times of distress. Specifically, I've structured each of the following chapters to help you seek God's face when you encounter uncertain periods in your life, such as anxiety, change, worry about your family and relationships, loneliness, health troubles, unanswered prayers, lost dreams, and more.

During times of hardship and pain, we find hope, comfort, and encouragement from our loving God. Yes, there is suffering in life—it is inescapable. But God is sovereign, and that is undeniable. He is our refuge and strength, a very present help in trouble. Whatever you're going through, remember that God has not forgotten you. You are not alone.

While tribulation is universal, it's temporary for the believer and it's surrounded by peace and cheer.

The apostle Peter, praising God for this truth, wrote,

Blessed be the God and Father of our Lord Jesus Christ, who according to His abundant mercy has begotten us again to a living hope through the resurrection of Jesus Christ from the dead . . . In this you greatly rejoice, though now for a little while, if need be, you have been grieved by various trials, that the genuineness of your faith, being much more precious than gold that perishes, though it is tested by fire, may be found to praise, honor, and glory at the revelation of Jesus Christ, whom having not seen you love. (1 Peter 1:3, 6–8)

If you're on stormy seas and being tossed about from the unexpected waves of daily living, remember this: You have a

While tribulation is universal,

it's temporary for the believer and

it's surrounded by peace and cheer.

Captain for your faith and an Anchor for your soul. If you're suffering from loss or illness and feeling helpless, know you have an Almighty Sovereign who sees and understands your heartache. If you have burdens that seem too heavy to bear, trust the Bible that is a "lamp unto your feet and a light unto your path" (119:105); it will guide and encourage you. And while your Bible also warns of tribulation and trials, it promises peace and good cheer.

Don't give up when the water is high and your faith feels weak. You are not alone! God has not forgotten you in your distress.

Call upon Him with the words of this hymn by Edward Hopper:

Jesus, Savior, pilot me
Over life's tempestuous sea;
Unknown waves before me roll,
Hiding rock and treacherous shoal.
Chart and compass come from Thee;
Jesus, Savior, pilot me.
As a mother stills her child,
Thou canst hush the ocean wild;
Boisterous waves obey Thy will
When Thou say'st to them, "Be still!"
Wondrous Sovereign of the sea,
Jesus, Savior, pilot me.[3]

One

You Are Not Forgotten

It was a case of David versus Goliath in the digital age. On one side of the fight was Google, the seemingly all-powerful tech giant bristling with lawyers and masses of corporate cash. On the other side was Mario Costeja González, a regular, everyday citizen of Spain.

What were these two combatants fighting about? The right to be forgotten.

One of the age-old "rules" of the internet is that anything posted online will remain online. Forever. That's because the archival and automatic save features of search engines (including Google) make it difficult, if not impossible, for pieces of content to ever really be deleted.

That reality became a big cause for concern for Mario Costeja González. All the way back in 1998, the Spanish Ministry of Labor and Public Affairs posted an article about landowners who were forced to sell their properties because of social security debts. The government wanted as many bidders as possible competing for those properties, so it publicized the list. Mr. González was one of the owners forced to sell.

Sixteen years later, in 2014, that article was still at the top of the search results whenever someone looked on Google for "Mario Costeja González." The old property had been disposed of long ago, and Mr. González's debts had not been an issue for more than a decade. But the article still haunted him. He couldn't get away from it. He tried to resolve the issue with Google through several channels, but nothing worked.

So Mario picked up his five smooth stones and prepared for a legal battle.

Amazingly, he won! The European Court of Justice ruled that Mr. González—and any other citizen of the European Union—did indeed possess the right to be forgotten. Meaning, they had the right to petition search engines to remove personal data that appeared to be inadequate or inaccurate, content that was no longer relevant, or content deemed excessive because of how much time had elapsed. Of course, there have been multiple layers of appeals since that initial ruling, and the practical consequences have taken years to play out. Still, the ruling was a major turning point in the history of the internet.[1]

There's an irony in that reality. All Mr. González wanted was the removal of a thirty-six-word article so he could move on from past troubles. By suing to make that happen, however, he has cemented his own legacy in connection with that fight.

In other words, because of his desire to be forgotten, Mario Costeja González will be remembered for decades or even centuries!

It's unlikely that you or I will take on a technology giant over the right to be forgotten. In fact, it's unlikely that you or I *want* to be forgotten.

Instead, most of us want to be remembered. We want to be remembered by our family and friends. We want to be remembered for our successes and our character. We want to be remembered for our accomplishments in this life, but most of all we want to be known and accepted by God. Our souls long for a deep relationship with the Creator of the universe, Almighty God.

The Good News of the Gospel is this: Through the death and resurrection of Jesus Christ, we have access to eternal life as a free gift received through faith. Because of God's Word, we can rest in the knowledge that God not only remembers us but also loves us and desires a relationship with us. It is His greatest desire that we live forever with Him in heaven.

Given those truths, why do we feel God is nowhere to be found? Why do we struggle with doubt about His care? And why is it easy to question whether He is listening to our cries for help?

Our souls long for a deep relationship with the Creator of the universe, Almighty God.

We'll address those questions throughout the pages of this book. And we'll do so primarily by focusing on the lives of different individuals in God's Word—starting with King David.

DAVID'S DISTRESS

As one of the most famous people in human history, David's story has been told and retold for centuries. As a young boy, the seventh son of seven sons, he was selected by God and appointed by the prophet Samuel to serve as the next king of Israel because the reigning king, Saul, had rebelled against God. After his anointing, David achieved national fame by volunteering to fight against a giant named Goliath and triumphing in God's name. Later he became a military leader for the army of Israel, eventually succeeding Saul as king of Israel.

Yet there are some details within David's narrative that are often passed over—the fifteen to twenty years between David's defeat of Goliath and his ascension to the throne—and many of those years were turbulent and challenging for David.

After David's victory over the giant, it's not surprising that the people loved him. They even sang songs about him: "Saul has slain his thousands, and David his ten thousands" (1 Samuel 18:7). As you might imagine, that kind of notoriety did not go over well with someone as narcissistic and paranoid as Saul. In this apprehensive state, Saul became jealous of David and determined to assassinate him. Ultimately David was forced to flee Jerusalem after Saul tried to kill him multiple times.

That was bad, but things got worse. After enjoying the luxury of Saul's palace, David spent years as a fugitive—sheltering in caves and spending innumerable nights under the open sky. He lived his life under constant threat from Saul and his soldiers.

These years were filled with relational strife as well. Incredibly, David's most faithful friend was Saul's son Jonathan—the prince and future king under the line of hereditary succession. Jonathan recognized David's anointing as the future king even if Saul never would or could. Adding to his personal strife, David was married to Saul's daughter. Can you imagine a more complicated personal scenario than that?

Take a moment to consider what David must have experienced during this time of exile as he reflected on his past life. His life started out so positively. As a young man, he was anointed as royalty. He demonstrated loyalty and bravery in fighting against Israel's enemies in God's name. He was beloved by an entire nation. But then everything changed. David was forced to abandon his family and flee, leaving behind his closest friend, or risk being murdered by that friend's father. Instead of life in the palace, he wandered in the wilderness for years to elude a murderous king.

Would it surprise you to learn that David felt like God had forgotten him? It's true. In the pain of that moment, David cried out to the Lord as he penned what we know today as Psalm 13:

> How long, O Lord? Will You forget me forever?
> How long will You hide Your face from me?
> How long shall I take counsel in my soul,
> Having sorrow in my heart daily?
> How long will my enemy be exalted over me?
> Consider and hear me, O Lord my God;
> Enlighten my eyes,
> Lest I sleep the sleep of death;
> Lest my enemy say,
> "I have prevailed against him";
> Lest those who trouble me rejoice when I am moved.
> But I have trusted in Your mercy;
> My heart shall rejoice in Your salvation.
> I will sing to the Lord,
> Because He has dealt bountifully with me. (vv. 1–6)

I understand what David was expressing in this psalm, and I expect you do as well. Haven't you asked those same questions? *How long, God? Will You forget me forever? Why are You hiding from me? Don't You care?*

Haven't you made those same declarations? *Remember me, God. Hear me, God. Show me something!*

Yet even in his distress, David showed us the antidote for those moments when it feels as if God is far away—even when it feels as if He has forgotten us completely.

HOPE IS THE ANTIDOTE FOR YOUR DISTRESS

In the midst of his pain, David reached out for consolation—and what he found was the truth of who God is and what He had done. "I have trusted in Your mercy," David wrote. "My heart shall rejoice in Your salvation. I will sing to the LORD, because He has dealt bountifully with me" (Psalm 13:5–6).

David focused on God's character, including His mercy, goodness, and sovereignty. And he remembered God's actions in the past—that God had saved David, blessed him, and been generous with him.

Because David knew and trusted in God and His nature, he found hope in the midst of his despair. You can find the same confidence even when it feels as if God has abandoned or forgotten you.

The truth is that every generation since Adam has faced

calamity. Within its epochs, the Bible records a long history of wars, plagues, famines, corruption, depravity, suffering, and wrongdoing. Yet God is in control. He reigns and rules and overrules. He has a plan; and when we walk with Him, we find ourselves lifted by the irresistible updraft of biblical hope.

The writer of Psalm 42 tapped into this when he wrote, "Why are you cast down, O my soul? And why are you disquieted within me? Hope in God, for I shall yet praise Him for the help of His countenance" (v. 5).

Dr. Martyn Lloyd-Jones, in commenting on this psalm, said,

> The first thing we have to learn is what the Psalmist learned—we must learn to take ourselves in hand. This man was not content just to lie down and commiserate with himself. He does something about it, he takes himself in hand. . . . He talks to himself. . . .
>
> I say that we must talk to ourselves instead of allowing "ourselves" to talk to us! Have you realized that most of your unhappiness in life is due to the fact that you are listening to yourself instead of talking to yourself?[2]

The good doctor is right. We need to speak truth to ourselves, and we need to encourage ourselves in the Lord. We must learn to search out and claim God's promises for our present needs and

God is in control.

He reigns and

rules and overrules.

future fears. We must ask the Holy Spirit to make those verses so real in our minds they'll lift our spirits like giant balloons of spiritual helium.

- The psalmist said, "I will hope continually, and will praise You yet more and more" (Psalm 71:14).
- Proverbs 10:28 says, "The hope of the righteous will be gladness."
- Jeremiah said, "Blessed is the man who trusts in the LORD, and whose hope is the LORD. For he shall be like a tree planted by the waters, which spreads out its roots by the river" (Jeremiah 17:7–8).
- Lamentations 3:21–26 says, "This I recall to my mind, therefore I have hope. . . . His compassions fail not. They are new every morning; great is Your faithfulness. 'The LORD is my portion,' says my soul, 'Therefore I hope in Him!' . . . It is good that one should hope and wait quietly."
- Romans 5:5 says, "Hope does not disappoint."
- The apostle Paul wrote, "Now may the God of hope fill you with all joy and peace in believing, that you may abound in hope by the power of the Holy Spirit" (Romans 15:13).

The Bible is filled with hopeful verses, and each one is special because God knows we sometimes feel hopeless. Peter said that we have been born again into a "living hope" (1 Peter 1:3). Romans 12:12 tells us to be "rejoicing in hope."

According to Isaiah 40, those who hope in the Lord shall renew their strength and mount up with wings like eagles. In a world where we're beset by burdens both big and small, we have the strong gusts of hope catching our wings and sending us soaring heavenward as God's hopeful, joyful people.

When it seems like God has forgotten you, turn to the only antidote that will cure what ails you: hope.

HOPE IS THE ANCHOR FOR YOUR SOUL

There is both good and bad news about the availability of hope. The good news is that the hope we have in God is free to all, and it is available in unlimited quantities. The bad news is that our confidence in that certain hope comes most easily when our lives are going smoothly. Hope is much more difficult to maintain when we are experiencing an emotional trial, which causes us, at times, to question if God has forgotten us.

Obviously, allowing our sense of hope to be determined by circumstances is no way to live. That's why the New Testament speaks of true hope being based on something immovable: the unchanging nature of God and the unchanging reality of His

Hope can actually

keep the soul from

being moved!

promises. The author of Hebrews was focused on those elements when he wrote, "This hope we have as an anchor of the soul, both sure and steadfast" (Hebrews 6:19).

I love that image: hope as the anchor of the soul. Hope can actually keep the soul from being moved!

Think about the gigantic Nimitz-class aircraft carriers in the US Navy. They carry two anchors that weigh thirty tons each and are held by chains in which every link weighs 360 pounds.[3] So when an aircraft carrier is anchored offshore, it has sixty tons of weight (even more counting the weight of the chains) protecting it from the movement of tide, wind, and waves.

That's an incredible image of the role hope plays in the human heart. Regardless of the winds and waves of circumstance that come against us, we can remain unmoved. We can be content; we can live with hope that God's promises are unchanged.

Our nation has an anchor: the founding documents of our Constitution and Bill of Rights, which were inspired by the Declaration of Independence. Those documents contain the core values and principles to which America returns whenever she faces crises—and there have been many in our history.

What about the anchor for the individual? Our founding document is God's Word, which contains the record of the unchanging nature and purposes of God for humanity. Specifically, the Bible contains the "exceedingly great and precious promises" (2 Peter

1:4), which the writer of Hebrews spoke about. God's promises are there to keep us firmly grounded as life's circumstances rise and fall around us. Circumstances will ebb and flow in our lives like waves on the seashore, but through it all our hope is anchored in God—hope based not on our emotions but on the Word of God.

The old saying goes, "If you can't face a problem, just turn around." The trouble with that philosophy is that problems keep recurring. Even if we ignore one for a time, another concern or trial will arise in the future. And it's always been that way.

Such is life. All it takes is an illness, a microscopic virus, an international incident, a natural disaster, or a change in political agendas to release a cascade of spark-like effects that ignite more troubles wherever they land.

David knew that to be true. He had enough problems to ignite an entire forest. Yet he also had an unshakable faith that God was with him—that God had not, and would not, forget about him. In that, David was correct. Though his time in the wilderness was long and filled with trials, it eventually came to an end. David was anointed as king in Jerusalem and ruled with passion and integrity for decades.

No, David was not perfect. Certainly he made his fair share of mistakes. Yet he never took his eyes off God's character, which is why he is known to this day as a man after God's own heart.

You and I can learn much from David and from his confidence in God's loving care. When we trust the way David trusted, we will say along with him, "I will sing to the LORD, because He has dealt bountifully with me" (Psalm 13:6).

Two

GOD HAS NOT FORGOTTEN YOU WHEN LIFE SEEMS UNCERTAIN

Eleven-year-old Hetty was sleeping soundly in her bed when, at 11:30 p.m., she was awakened by something falling on her blanket. It was pieces of the ceiling and the roof above—and they were on fire! Bolting from her bed, Hetty rushed to find her father, Samuel.

Unknown to Hetty, her father had already been awakened by a commotion outside—someone was yelling, "Fire!" Not realizing it was his own house that was burning, Samuel had risen to investigate. Opening the door of the room, he was confronted by flames in the hallway.

The house was a wooden structure, and the flames were consuming it quickly. The roof was imploding into the second-floor rooms as Samuel and his wife, Susanna, frantically tried to gather their eight children and escape. (One other child, Samuel Jr., was away at school.)

Susanna was pregnant and had been sleeping in a different room from her husband because she felt unwell. She escaped down the stairs with her two oldest daughters. A live-in servant broke an upstairs window and escaped with Hetty and another sibling. Another servant rushed to the nursery to get one-year-old Charles and five-year-old Jacky. Scooping up Charles, the servant told Jacky to follow her and headed for the hallway and stairs. But when she arrived in the garden, little Jacky was nowhere to be seen. He had started out of the room behind the nurse but turned back when he saw the flames.

Samuel attempted several times to reach young Jacky, but he could not penetrate the flames. Convinced they had lost their son, the family prayed and asked God to receive his soul.

But the outcome was far better. Jacky had retreated back into his room and gone to the window, where he was seen by members of the crowd below. With no ladder at hand, one man stood on another's shoulders and reached up, pulling Jacky through the window to safety. The house and all the family's possessions were a total loss. Yet something far greater was saved—a husband, a wife, and their children.

As the flames consumed their home, Samuel called out to the

crowd: "Come, neighbors! Let us kneel down! Let us give thanks to God! He has given me all my eight children. Let the house go—I am rich enough!"[1]

That night, he could not have known how prophetic his words were. Not only did God give Samuel and Susanna Wesley all their children despite the flames, He gave the church two of her most powerful voices: Charles and John "Jacky" Wesley. Being saved from that fire had a profound impact on five-year-old John Wesley. His mother, Susanna, would subsequently refer to John as a "brand plucked from the burning," a reference to Zechariah 3:2: "Is this not a brand plucked from the fire?"[2]

If you're familiar with John Wesley as a historical figure, you know his life was full of ups and downs. His father was an Anglican priest and his mother was diligent in teaching her children spiritual truths. John himself joined the Anglican church as a priest, even sailing to the New World, America, to serve as a pastor to British colonists in Georgia. Yet he struggled with doubt and was at times deeply aware of his own hypocrisy and lack of faith. Wesley stumbled into forming a new denomination, the Methodist Church, without ever intending to do so. Even as his movement grew, Wesley and his followers became victims of persecution by the official Church of England, which escalated into physical attacks.

Throughout these ups and downs, John Wesley carried a

"Let us give thanks to God! He has given me all my eight children. Let the house go—I am rich enough!"

sense within himself that God had rescued him from his family's burning house for a purpose. Even during the downs, he felt a strong sense of God's presence and ultimate direction in his life.

As we've seen already in these pages—and as you have no doubt experienced in your personal journey—life is filled with uncertainty. It plays out on a grand scale through wars and strife, natural disasters, poverty, pandemics, and more. But it also plays out in each of our stories through relational conflict, work shortages, sickness, emotional trauma, and the like.

Despite these realities of daily living, we can carry the same sense of God's presence and purpose that sustained John Wesley through his many trials. We know this because God has promised to never leave us or forsake us.

JOB WAS CRUSHED BY TRAGEDY

One of the main sources of uncertainty in our lives is that we don't always experience the kind of rescue young John Wesley received. Sometimes we have to face the fire. And sometimes we get burned.

Looking at God's Word, no one understood that reality better or more bitterly than Job.

Like David's, Job's story is familiar even to those who do

not follow Christ. He is a historical figure and an archetype of human suffering. Yet even if you have read Job's story many times, I encourage you to approach it once more with a focus on Job not as a lesson—but as a person.

It was a day like any other day, which means Job had been up early to offer sacrifices to God on behalf of his ten children (Job 1:5). He managed his business as usual, giving directions to his various servants. He ate a meal with his wife. He went about his life as if everything were normal—right until tragedy struck.

The first wave was difficult: "A messenger came to Job and said, 'The oxen were plowing and the donkeys feeding beside them, when the Sabeans raided *them* and took them away—indeed they have killed the servants with the edge of the sword; and I alone have escaped to tell you!'" (vv. 14–15).

Now, it's easy for modern readers to look at these verses and think, *Job lost some animals. What's the big deal?* But that's not an accurate perspective for the ancient world. Oxen and donkeys were the industrial machines of Job's day. They were necessary for plowing fields and other important jobs, which made losing them similar to a farmer losing his tractor or a delivery driver losing her truck. Not only that, but the Sabean raiders also murdered Job's servants. These were people Job knew and cared for.

The second and third waves were just as troubling: "While he was still speaking, another also came and said, 'The fire of God fell from heaven and burned up the sheep and the servants, and consumed them; and I alone have escaped to tell you!' While he was still speaking, another also came and said, 'The Chaldeans formed three bands, raided the camels and took them away, yes, and killed the servants with the edge of the sword; and I alone have escaped to tell you!'" (vv. 16–17).

Once again, these were critical losses for Job—the servants first and foremost. Human beings who looked to Job as a master and provider had been slaughtered, and that knowledge must have cut Job to the core. But don't overlook the loss of the sheep and camels as well. In the ancient world, herds were more than pets or profit. They represented generational wealth. A healthy and growing herd of sheep or cattle would provide not only for Job's needs in the present day but also for his children and grand-children long into the future. Now that provision had been cut short. It was as if Job's entire retirement plan had turned to ash.

Can you see Job as a person in that moment? His friends and workers had been killed. His livelihood was destroyed. His financial security was in ruins. Can you imagine how his thoughts were reeling? Or perhaps he was struck numb by the rapid-fire delivery of bad news and simply collapsed into a ball on the ground.

Alas, the fourth wave was worst of all: "While he was still speaking, another also came and said, 'Your sons and daughters were eating and drinking wine in their oldest brother's house, and suddenly a great wind came from across the wilderness and struck the four corners of the house, and it fell on the young people, and they are dead; and I alone have escaped to tell you!'" (vv. 18–19).

Any parent who has lost a child knows the pain is unthinkable. Unendurable. Job lost all ten of his children in the same moment. He must have felt as if his own heart were crushed underneath that fallen home.

Yes, Job understood the pain of uncertainty, of tragedy. Yet as we'll see, he also understood the best way to respond in such moments.

CHAOS CREATES QUESTIONS

If I had to summarize the human response to tragedy in a single word, I would choose a short one: *Why?*

Of course, people respond to chaos and tragedy in different ways. Many rant and rail with anger. Others sink to their knees with grief or retreat into isolation. Still others pretend the problem doesn't exist or contend that it's not important.

In the end, though, each of those reactions will lead back to that simple, one-syllable question. *Why?*

That word has been part of our lives for as long as we can remember. It's one of the first words we learn—just ask any parent whose child is in the *why?* phase. It's the word teenagers use when they begin questioning authority and demand justification for rules. It's one of the questions we ask during life's final stages in the hospice or sick room. It's the query of philosophers, the mystery of theologians, and the confounding of humanity throughout history.

Why? is also a biblical question. As we read about the heroes of Scripture, we often find this word on their lips:

- Moses prayed, "Lord, *why* have You brought trouble on this people? *Why* is it You have sent me?" (Exodus 5:22, emphasis added).
- Joshua cried, "Alas, Lord GOD, *why* have You brought this people over the Jordan at all—to deliver us into the hand of the Amorites, to destroy us?" (Joshua 7:7, emphasis added).
- David prayed, "*Why* are You so far from helping Me, and from the words of My groaning?" (Psalm 22:1, emphasis added).
- Isaiah asked, "O LORD, *why* have You made us stray from Your ways?" (Isaiah 63:17, emphasis added).
- Jeremiah mourned, "*Why* have You stricken us so that there is no healing for us?" (Jeremiah 14:19, emphasis added).

- And Jesus cried out on the cross, saying, "My God, My God, *why* have You forsaken Me?" (Matthew 27:46, emphasis added).

The chaos and uncertainty Job experienced resulted in many questions from his lips as well—most of them directed toward God. In fact, the book of Job is filled with questions. Every chapter, except two (chapters 29 and 32), contains at least one question mark, and Job asked "Why?" a combined twenty-nine times.

OUR QUESTIONS HAVE ANSWERS

Right now you may be thinking, *I've heard enough about questions. I know what it's like to ask questions. What I need is answers!*

In such moments, it's critical that you recognize your own limitations. If you don't have answers in moments of uncertainty, don't double down on your own intelligence or your own solutions. Don't waste energy complaining to those around you or medicating your sorrows with self-pity.

Instead, turn to the One who can answer any question and already knows exactly what you're experiencing and precisely what you need. That's what Job did.

Even though Job had far more questions than answers, he kept affirming and reaffirming his faith.

- "The LORD gave, and the LORD has taken away; blessed be the name of the LORD" (1:21).
- "Shall we indeed accept good from God, and shall we not accept adversity?" (2:10).
- "Though He slay me, yet will I trust Him" (13:15).
- "I know that my Redeemer lives, and He shall stand at last on the earth; and after my skin is destroyed, this I know, that in my flesh I shall see God" (19:25–26).
- "He knows the way that I take; when He has tested me, I shall come forth as gold" (23:10).

In the opening narrative of Job, God shows us as readers the *reason* Job was being attacked. Satan was accusing him before God in the realms of heaven, and God allowed the enemy to persecute Job as a test of his faith. In the last chapter, we're told the *results* of Job's sorrows and the blessings that crowned the last half of his years, which Job experienced only after his suffering.

Importantly, Job did not have access to any of that information. He did not understand the *why*, and he had no concept of what was to come. As a result, chapters 3 to 41 record Job and his friends attempting to work through his emotions and circumstances based on that limited knowledge.

Despite his lack of information, Job consistently turned his questions and his energy toward God. Job understood that God alone could provide the answers he longed to receive.

Like Job, we seldom understand the reasons behind the uncertainty we face. We are rarely given access to the *why*. Yet that shouldn't prevent us from trusting that God has answers to our questions and that He will reveal them in His good timing. Indeed, our lack of answers should drive us to our Savior!

The truth is that our faith shines brightest during adversity. Without adversity there's little need for faith. If our faith doesn't work in the darkness, it's not much good in the light. And so I challenge you even in moments of tragedy to actively and consciously trust in God, knowing that someday you'll understand it all.

He is the Answer to the uncertainty of life.

Three

GOD HAS NOT FORGOTTEN YOU WHEN YOU FEEL ANXIOUS

As the starting quarterback for the Dallas Cowboys, Dak Prescott had a lot going for him heading into the 2020 season. For starters, he signed a contract that would pay him $31.4 million for a single year. In addition, Prescott's team had a good chance of competing for the playoffs in the NFC East division, and possibly contending for the Super Bowl.

That's why it came as a surprise when Prescott revealed before the first game of the year that he had received treatment in the off-season for anxiety and depression.

The primary cause of Prescott's illness was the recent death of his older brother, Jace, who committed suicide. "Tears and tears and tears," Prescott said of the moment he received the news. "I mean, I sat there and tried to gather what had happened and wanted to ask why for so many reasons."

Another contributor to his depression was the isolation Prescott experienced during the COVID-19 pandemic. "I'm somebody that likes to be around people. I like to inspire. I like to put a smile on people's faces, day in and day out, and I like to lead. When that's taken away from you simply because you're forced to quarantine and not be around people and get around people as much as you would like to, yeah, it's tough."

Many people view anxiety and depression as a stigma—as something to keep private because it makes you look incapable or weak. This is especially true within the church. Followers of Christ often have a difficult time admitting they need help with anxiety or other mental disorders because they fear such incidents will make them seem spiritually deficient. They worry that others will view them as lacking in faith or failing to have a deep connection with God.

Given these realities, Prescott's bravery in speaking publicly about his experiences should be commended. "I don't want to sit here and dwell on the things that were a struggle for me when I know I'm very fortunate and blessed and other people have it much worse," he told the interviewer. "But [it's important] just to be transparent about it—that even in my situation, emotions and

"Emotions and those type of things can overcome you if you don't do something about it."

those type of things can overcome you if you don't do something about it."[1]

Prescott was right to draw attention to anxiety and depression, because the numbers surrounding those issues are astounding. Studies show that nearly 20 percent of adult Americans suffer from an anxiety disorder in a given year—which is about forty-one million people. That number jumps to almost three hundred million people worldwide.[2] Perhaps most alarming is that incidents of anxiety among younger people have been rising for years.

Interestingly, if you think anxiety and depression are modern phenomena that have only begun affecting people in recent decades, you're mistaken. We know those issues have plagued people for centuries because of what we read in the pages of Scripture.

ANXIETY IN SCRIPTURE

There are many mistaken beliefs regarding scriptural content. One misconception is that God's Word is a collection of historical stories and other writings designed to communicate doctrine. In other words, many people see the Bible primarily as a source of information.

In reality, the Bible is God's revelation of Himself. It is a source of inspiration, not just information. Through it God demonstrates not only His character but who He is and what He values. It goes well beyond transmitting information—it illustrates the highs and lows we experience on this earthly journey as well as God's never-ending love for us.

The book of Psalms is considered the emotional heart of God's Word. In its collection of 150 songs and poems, the authors poured out their thoughts, tapping into deep mines of joy, sorrow, thankfulness, anger, praise, doubt, worship, disgust, love, misery, pride, loneliness, and yes, anxiety.

For example, look at David's eye-opening appeal to God at the beginning of Psalm 69:

> Save me, O God!
> For the waters have come up to my neck.
> I sink in deep mire,
> Where there is no standing;
> I have come into deep waters,
> Where the floods overflow me.
> I am weary with my crying;
> My throat is dry;
> My eyes fail while I wait for my God. (vv. 1–3)

There may not be a better visual description for anxiety than someone beginning to panic as the waters rise up to their neck and threaten to engulf them completely—of sinking into a muck and mire so slick and sludgy that "there is no standing."

If you read Psalm 69 in its entirety, you'll see that it is packed with emotion. David speaks of his "shame," his "crying," and his "sorrowful" state. He runs the gamut from crying out to God for salvation all the way to angrily urging God to strike down those who have reproached and opposed him.

Yet in the midst of this outpouring of emotion, David still clung to the solid rock of God's nature and character. "But as for me, my prayer is to You," he wrote. "O LORD, in the acceptable time; O God, in the multitude of Your mercy, hear me in the truth of Your salvation" (v. 13).

Later he added,

> Hear me, O LORD, for Your lovingkindness is good;
> Turn to me according to the multitude of Your tender mercies.
> And do not hide Your face from Your servant,
> For I am in trouble;
> Hear me speedily.
> Draw near to my soul, and redeem it;
> Deliver me because of my enemies. (vv. 16–18)

David understood the solution for anxiety was not to try to solve all the problems that were making him feel anxious. The solution was not to strike out against his enemies with royal authority or a warrior's blade. Instead, David knew the only way to resolve the anxiety within himself was to turn it over to God.

Psalm 80 is another example of a biblical writer experiencing the same emotions as the rest of us. In it, the psalmist expressed both his anxiety about the decline of Israel and his indignation that God was not acting to save or restore His people.

"Give ear, O Shepherd of Israel, You who lead Joseph like a flock; You who dwell between the cherubim, shine forth! Before Ephraim, Benjamin, and Manasseh, stir up Your strength, and come and save us!" (vv. 1–2).

Remember feeling worried about the decline of your nation? Or your community? Or your family? Can you recall the help-lessness of that situation? The desire to see someone, anyone, take action that would result in change? The psalmist felt the same way as he watched Israel's spiritual and economic decline. Yet he understood that only God could intervene—so why didn't He?

In a wonderful poetic expression, the psalmist used the metaphor of a vine and vineyard to describe Israel's state. He described a tiny plant rescued out of Egypt that had grown strong with roots filling the land from the sea to the Jordan River. Yet recently that vineyard had begun to collapse. The walls were

David knew the only way to resolve the anxiety within himself was to turn it over to God.

broken down. People traveling on the road would reach out to pluck its fruit. The animals were devouring it from end to end.

Once again, the psalmist understood that the solution to his anxiety was not coming up with his own plans for the restoration of Israel. The answer was not stirring up the people to act more spiritually or obey more rules. Instead, the psalmist cried out for God to move and work a miracle within His vineyard—within His special people.

"Restore us, O Lord God of hosts," he wrote. "Cause Your face to shine, and we shall be saved!" (v. 19).

As you read through the psalms, you will discover authors inspired by the Holy Spirit who experienced the same sources of anxiety we experience today—sickness, decline, financial woes, enemies at the door, and more. Yet again and again, those same authors poured out their worry and their anxious thoughts to God rather than deny those feelings or seek solace elsewhere.

As a result, they found peace.

ANXIETY IN OUR LIVES

What causes anxiety in our lives today? Anxiety instigators are too numerous to count, but a recent article on WebMD narrowed them down to fourteen common sources, including:

- panic disorders;
- phobias;
- stress from work;
- stress from school;
- illness and other medical conditions;
- difficulties in our personal relationships, including marriage;
- financial pressure;
- unpredictable world events or conflicts;
- emotional trauma;
- side effects of medication or illicit drugs;
- and more.[3]

Looking at that list through the lens of my experiences as a pastor, I have found that finances, relationships, and illness are more often than not key contributors to the soaring levels of anxiety in our society today.

Of course, everyone gets anxious about their financial condition at some point. That is true for churchgoers and non-churchgoers. It's true for both younger and older people. It's true for Republicans and Democrats and any other demographic you can come up with to divide people into groups. Unfortunately, simply acquiring more money doesn't solve the problem. Yes, even wealthy people are anxious about money!

Relationships are ever present in our lives, and most often they are beneficial to our lives and well-being. After all, we are designed to live in relationships—both with other people and with our Creator. However, the very fact that relationships are so critical in our lives can cause great amounts of stress and worry when those relationships become troubled or turn sour. The simple truth is that people have the ability to hurt others. Therefore, even as we develop the depth we desire in our closest relationships, we open ourselves up to greater feelings of hurt and anger and betrayal if the relationship fails in some way.

Finally, sickness is an ever-present source of anxiety because it can strike at any moment. This is especially true for those of us traveling through the second half of our lives. No matter how well we are doing financially, how deeply we share life with our children and grandchildren, or how much we enjoy the fellowship of our community and our local church—people today are constantly aware of the shadow of unexpected illness. And when we fall under that shadow, it can cause anxiety to rise unexpectedly.

Money, relationships, and illness. The bad news is that all three of those anxiety inducers are critical elements of human life. We can't avoid them. They will always be with us.

The good news is there is a solution. Specifically, I'd like to offer a three-point answer to dealing with any anxiety you may be feeling.

1. Be Utterly Dependent on God

One key to dealing with anxiety is to remember that, although unwelcome, stress and adversity propel us to new levels of faith, teaching us to be utterly dependent on God. The Bible promises that God will meet the needs of His children, so in *every* circumstance we can trust in His provision (Philippians 4:19). Jesus reminds us not to worry about our lives, what we will eat or drink, but to look at the birds and the lilies of the field, for the God who makes provision for them cares even more for us (Matthew 6:25–30). And the psalmist affirms God's watchful care for us with these words: "I have been young, and now am old; yet I have not seen the righteous forsaken, nor his descendants begging bread" (Psalm 37:25).

What do these verses show us? God is faithful in every situation! We need to depend on Him as our ultimate help in trouble—He knows and cares about our needs.

Sometimes financial panic is actually a gale that pushes us onto the shores of trusting in God's faithfulness. In 1871, a YMCA convention was held in Carlisle, Pennsylvania, with many Christian business leaders present. Presiding was John Wanamaker, the famous retailer known today as the father of modern advertising. On the second day of the conference, a telegram arrived with shocking news. The banking house of Jay Cooke & Company had failed, resulting in terrible losses

Sometimes financial panic is actually a gale that pushes us onto the shores of trusting in God's faithfulness.

for Wanamaker and for others at the convention. Soon reports flowed in of other firms failing and of a nationwide financial crash. A feeling of panic swept the convention, making it hard to conduct business or to continue the proceedings.

One of the delegates, Erastus Johnson, came across Psalm 61:2: "From the end of the earth I will cry to You, when my heart is overwhelmed; lead me to the rock that is higher than I." Based on that verse, Johnson wrote a song that was instantly put to music at the convention and sung repeatedly. It became a favorite hymn of its day, and it's still good for us now:

> *Oh! Sometimes the shadows are deep,*
> *And rough seems the path to the goal,*
> *And sorrows, sometimes how they sweep*
> *Like tempests down over the soul.*
> *O then to the Rock let me fly,*
> *To the Rock that is higher than I.*
> *O then to the Rock let me fly,*
> *To the Rock that is higher than I!*[4]

You can stand on the Rock without a penny in your pocket, without a dollar in your account, without an expectation for an answer. He'll provide in His own time and way.

The same is true for our relationships and our health. We can trust God with all our needs. He who spared not His own Son but freely gave Him for us all, will He not also give us all things we need (Romans 8:32)? Therefore, choose to be utterly dependent on Him—He will be with us through whatever adversity we encounter in life—"For He Himself has said, 'I will never leave you nor forsake you'" (Hebrews 13:5).

2. Be Rich in Good Deeds

The Bible also tells us to be content with whatever we have, though it be little, and to be rich in good deeds. The words of 1 Timothy 6:6–8 seem to have been written with today's headlines in mind: "Godliness with contentment is great gain. For we brought nothing into this world, and it is certain we can carry nothing out. And having food and clothing, with these we shall be content."

The passage warns about the dangers of loving money too much, and then adds, "Command those who are rich in this present age not to be haughty, nor to trust in uncertain riches but in the living God, who gives us richly all things to enjoy. Let them do good, that they be rich in good works, ready to give, willing to share, storing up for themselves a good foundation for the time to come" (vv. 17–19).

What practical advice for the times we live in! Be content. Enjoy what you have. Be rich in good works.

Be content. Enjoy what you have. Be rich in good works.

Once again, these principles have a similar application with our relationships and our health. Yes, our interactions with others can become a constant source of anxiety—but that usually happens when we are thinking about ourselves. Most often we become stressed when we think others aren't meeting our needs or our expectations. We can shed our anxiety by focusing on the needs of others and being generous in our relationships.

That is true also for our physical and mental health. Yes, there will be times when we experience illness, but there will also be seasons of health and strength and vitality! Make the choice to serve others and sow joy when you are able, and when you are ill, others will sow blessings into your life.

Job said he came into the world naked and would leave it the same way, and Paul said we brought nothing into the world and will take nothing out. But there is one investment we can make now that will last throughout eternity: We can lay up treasures in heaven (Matthew 6:19–21). When we are rich in good deeds, we create an investment that will never lose its value and will pay eternal dividends.

3. Be Focused on Spiritual Wealth

Another good Bible study for anxious times is found in Ephesians. In chapters 1 through 3, the apostle Paul provides an inventory of our endless, everlasting wealth as children of God and citizens of His kingdom. The words *rich* and *riches* occur six times in these chapters, and all six verses are worth memorizing on the asset side of our mental ledger.

Here are the highlights:

- "In Him we have redemption through His blood, the forgiveness of sins, according to the riches of His grace" (1:7).
- "The riches of the glory of His inheritance in the saints" (1:18).
- "God, who is rich in mercy . . ." (2:4).
- "In the ages to come He might show the exceeding riches of His grace in His kindness toward us in Christ Jesus" (2:7).
- "The unsearchable riches of Christ . . ." (3:8).
- "That He would grant you, according to the riches of His glory, to be strengthened with might through His Spirit in the inner man" (3:16).

In John 14, Jesus offers assurance of our future home—He is preparing a mansion for us in heaven. And Revelation 21–22 describes a diamond city with golden streets, translucent walls, crystal waters, and a glorious throne—our eternal inheritance in Him, for we are heirs of God and coheirs with Christ. Best of all, this inheritance "can never perish, spoil or fade. This inheritance is kept in heaven for you" (1 Peter 1:4 NIV). This is the wealth that "neither moth nor rust destroys and where thieves do not break in and steal" (Matthew 6:20). We can fall asleep at night knowing that our eternal inheritance is secure because we know and have accepted Jesus as our Lord and Savior.

Who can measure the joy we will experience in our heavenly home? We will spend eternity with the people most dear to us in a place devoid of tears, anger, pain, pressure, betrayal, or any other source of conflict that creates relational stress and strife. Yes, there will be anxious moments between you and those you love here on earth, but when you focus on the immense joy we will experience for all eternity, those moments will fade in importance.

Physically, we can trust God's promise that our last breath in this world will lead immediately to strong lungs filled with the sweetest air imaginable in the next. That's because we have been promised not just new bodies in heaven but new glorified bodies that are as eternal as our resurrected Savior: "For we know that if our earthly house, this tent, is destroyed, we have a building from God, a house not made with hands, eternal in the heavens" (2 Corinthians 5:1).

Here is the reality we must face about our world: We can't effectively insure ourselves against financial loss. There are no truly safe investments, and who knows what the future will hold? With nations teetering on top of mountains of debt, who knows how serious the next economic crisis will be, or when a recession could become a depression?

We can trust God's promise that our last breath in this world will lead immediately to strong lungs filled with the sweetest air imaginable in the next.

Thankfully, there is a spiritual reality we can count on during times of need. Namely, nothing depresses our Lord, and there's never a run on heaven's bank. He tells us, "Let not your heart be troubled, neither let it be afraid" (John 14:27).

Place your dependence on Him, be rich in good deeds, turn your thoughts toward eternal investments, and don't feel forsaken; for whatever your current circumstances are, you have this assurance: God has not forgotten you. He will take care of you.

Four

God Has Not Forgotten You When Times Change

It's been said many times that people don't like change. In my experience, however, I have not found that to be the case. Many people enjoy a change of scenery when they take a vacation or move to a new place. People like technological changes when they benefit from them. And everyone is pleased when their financial circumstances change for the better.

No, it's not that people don't like change. We simply don't like changes that are outside our control.

I can show you what I mean by stating two simple words: *pink slip.* Aren't those two terrifying words? Nobody enjoys that kind of change!

Interestingly, we don't know who coined the phrase "pink slip," but it seems to date to the turn of the twentieth century, when most employees were still paid in cash. Each week's wages came in an envelope, and anyone being laid off that week would find a notice—usually on pink paper—in the envelope along with their final wages. *Random House Dictionary* dated the earliest reference to the phrase all the way back to the early 1900s, so it's been part of our language for more than one hundred years.

Few people today get an actual pink slip, but that doesn't mean people don't still lose their employment—along with the loss of security, confidence, and esteem that comes with their termination notice.

Since the year 2000, Americans have experienced the whiplash effects of a roller-coaster economy. The great tech run-up of the 1990s drove the economy and markets sky-high and brought jobs with that expansion. But the markets crashed in 2000, millions of jobs were lost, and the search for new opportunities began again. By 2008, it looked like there was no end to the real estate boom and the increases in employment it brought—until the end came, and we entered the biggest recession since the Great Depression.

The markets and economy began slowly expanding again in 2009, setting off the longest bull market seen for decades. But in early 2020, the COVID-19 pandemic struck, throwing the economy into an unexpected downward spiral. Millions of people lost their jobs. Trillions of dollars were printed and spent by the federal government to provide some sustenance to struggling companies and households. Tens of thousands of businesses—mostly small, but some very large—closed their doors for good. And millions of Americans searched for new ways to redefine their role in the marketplace, looking for opportunities to provide for their families.

How do we respond to that kind of change? I'm talking about change that shakes us and turns our world upside down. Change that causes fear and frustration. Changes in our circumstances that force us to reexamine ourselves and evaluate what might be changing in our own heart and mind. In the face of such challenges, how can we not wonder whether God has forgotten about us?

It starts by changing our focus—by not looking at our circumstances or ourselves—and zeroing in on God.

REMEMBER THAT GOD NEVER CHANGES

The best way to deal with difficult changes in your life is to remember that *God never changes* and to refocus your attention and energy on Him.

How do we know God does not change? Because of Scripture:

- Through the prophet Malachi, God reminded the Israelites that their continuation as a people was dependent on God's stability: "For I am the LORD, I do not change; therefore you are not consumed, O sons of Jacob" (Malachi 3:6).
- The book of Numbers made the same claim through rhetorical questions: "God is not a man, that He should lie, nor a son of man, that He should repent. Has He said, and will He not do? Or has He spoken, and will He not make it good?" (23:19).
- The author of Hebrews was more direct, simply stating, "Jesus Christ is the same yesterday, today, and forever" (13:8).
- And the apostle James wrote, "Every good gift and every perfect gift is from above, and comes down from the Father of lights, with whom there is no variation or shadow of turning" (1:17).

The message is clear: God does not change. Yet you may be wondering, *What does that mean for me? How does God's character help me when my life is changing more quickly than I can keep up?*

As an answer, think of a compass. Because they are mainly used for outdoor activities, compasses can typically take a lot of punishment. You might drop one in a stream or a river, for example, and send it tumbling along with the current for miles. Or you might drop one during a mountain hike and watch it bounce and skitter down the slope.

Yet no matter what you do to that compass—no matter how much you shake it, drop it, drag it, spin it, or throw it—when you open the lid and look at the face, it will still point you to true north. In other words, changing circumstances don't affect a compass's distinguishing feature.

North is still north.

Similarly, *your* changing circumstances don't affect *God's* character. And for that reason, you can rely on God to guide you through those circumstances even when everything in your life seems shaken and stirred.

God is still God. He is the Rock of stability to which you can anchor when everything else is uncertain. Because He has not forgotten you.

REALIZE THAT GOD GUIDES US

Not only is God unchanging in His character, but He actively guides us through the circumstances of our lives. Once again, Scripture reveals that truth:

Your changing circumstances
don't affect God's character.

- Proverbs 3:5–6 promises that as we trust the Lord with all our hearts and acknowledge Him in all our ways, He will guide us in all our paths.
- Psalm 23 says our Shepherd will lead us in the right paths.
- Isaiah wrote, "Thus says the Lord . . . I am the Lord your God, who teaches you to profit, who leads you by the way you should go" (48:17).

Perhaps the best visual reminder of God's guidance occurs in the book of Numbers. In chapter 9, God's leadership among the children of Israel took visible shape in the form of a mysterious cloud, which at night turned into a pillar of fire:

> Now on the day that the tabernacle was raised up, the cloud covered the tabernacle, the tent of the Testimony; from evening until morning it was above the tabernacle like the appearance of fire. So it was always: the cloud covered it by day, and the appearance of fire by night. Whenever the cloud was taken up from above the tabernacle, after that the children of Israel would journey; and in the place where the cloud settled, there the children of Israel would pitch their tents. (vv. 15–17)

Whenever the cloud lifted from above the tent, the Israelites set out; whenever it settled, the Israelites camped. When the cloud remained over the tabernacle a long time, the Israelites obeyed the Lord's order and did not set out. Sometimes the cloud was over the tabernacle only a few days; sometimes only one night; sometimes a year. But whether by day or by night, whenever the cloud lifted, the people packed their belongings quickly and followed after.

Once again you might object, thinking, *That was great for the Israelites, but what about me? Where is my cloud when I need God to guide me?*

It's true that we no longer have God's visible cloud above us, but we do have His invisible Spirit within us and His infallible Word in our hands. We have His providential ordering of our circumstances and His promise to direct us in all our ways.

If we seem stuck for the moment, even if it appears to be for a prolonged period, we're better off remaining stuck in God's will than wandering off on our own. Sometimes we can make a lot of progress when we're standing still, though it doesn't appear so at the time.

For these reasons, if you are walking according to God's will, don't focus on the pace of change. Don't become overwhelmed by the presence of change. Take one day at a time, do your best, and let Him lead you by His divine agenda.

The Lord knows the way through the wilderness.

If we seem stuck . . . we're better
off remaining stuck in God's will
than wandering off on our own.

REDIRECT TO THE NEXT LOGICAL STEP

When we encounter times of extreme change in our lives, the first step is to refocus on God's unchanging character; He is our compass that will not fail. The second step is to remember that God actively guides us; we can trust His direction.

Of course, in the midst of drastic change, it's difficult to simply stop and stand still until God reveals His entire plan for the next several years. In fact, God rarely reveals His plans or His directions to us in that way. Instead, He often uncovers only the next stage in our journey without revealing His final destination.

Therefore, the final step to take during periods of extreme change involves redirecting our thoughts and actions toward what God has already revealed.

The Israelites experienced such a moment when they camped on the shores of the Red Sea after their exodus from Egypt. In his book *The Red Sea Rules*, Rob Morgan points out that on the shores of that sea, the Israelites couldn't see into the distance. They had no binoculars that could view Canaan, nor even the opposite shore. But the Lord gave them a simple plan: "Tell the children of Israel to go forward" (Exodus 14:15).[1]

The old commentator C. H. Mackintosh had an interesting view about this moment. He believed the Red Sea did not open up

God often uncovers only the next stage in our journey without revealing His final destination.

across the entire expanse all at once but rather opened progressively as Israel moved forward, so they needed to trust God for each fresh step. Mackintosh wrote, "God never gives guidance for two steps at a time. I must take one step, and then I get light for the next. This keeps the heart in abiding dependence upon God."[2]

I find it interesting that Moses and the Israelites knew their promised land—the land full of milk and honey—was located in Canaan. Yet when God led the people out of Egypt, instead of going straight north into Canaan, they turned south into the Sinai Desert. Obviously, the people were confused by the diversion, but there was a reason. The warlike Philistines inhabited the land between Egypt and Canaan. If the unskilled and untrained Hebrew nation had encountered them, they likely would have been soundly defeated, and those who survived would have fled back to safety in Egypt.

So Moses led them south toward the Red Sea and Sinai (Exodus 13:17–18). In doing so, he saved their lives and provided an opportunity for them to witness God's miracle of parting the waters of the Red Sea.

The same is true when we experience periods of massive change. When our lives are diverted in an unexpected direction, we have no way of knowing God's purpose at that moment. Sometimes those radical changes can reveal things we never would have seen otherwise—if only we will be patient and trust God's leading.

Missionary Isobel Kuhn learned that lesson when the Communists overran China in the 1940s. Aware of the danger she was in, Isobel escaped the country on foot with her young son, Danny, by traveling across the dangerous, snow-covered Pienma Pass. She finally arrived at Myitkyina in Upper Burma (Myanmar), but there she was stranded at what felt like the end of the world without money, unable to speak the language, and still half a globe away from home. "I cannot tell you the dismay and alarm that filled me," she later wrote.

Despite her perplexity, Isobel made two decisions in that moment of unforeseen, unwanted change. "The first thing is to cast out fear," she said. "The only fear a Christian should entertain is the fear of sin. All other fears are from Satan, sent to confuse and weaken us. How often the Lord reiterated to His disciples, 'Be not afraid!'" So, Isobel knelt and spread her heart before her Lord. "I refused to be afraid and asked Him to cast such fears out of my heart."

Isobel's second determination was to "seek light for the next step." She had no idea how to get out of Asia, but with God's help she believed she could figure out what to do that day to find some food and funds, to find a safe place to stay, and to find a means of communicating with the outside world. Meaning, Isobel did the next right and reasonable thing. Instead of waiting on God's entire plan to be revealed, she took what steps she could with what light she had.

"The first thing is to cast out fear.
The only fear a Christian should
entertain is the fear of sin."

In time, she arrived back home, safe and sound. Her salvation came not by waiting until she knew exactly what to do in every situation, but by trusting God for guidance in small increments, taking the journey one footprint at a time.[3]

The same strategy works when you experience unforeseen, unwanted change. When you don't know what to do next, cast out fear and seek light for the next step. Trust God for guidance in small increments. And if you can't see what lies dimly in the distance, do what lies clearly at hand.

Five

GOD HAS NOT FORGOTTEN YOU
WHEN YOUR FAMILY IS HURTING

It was a typical October day for Dr. Earl McQuay—until it wasn't.

Dr. McQuay gave a morning lecture to his seminary students at Columbia International University in South Carolina. The subject was the stages of grief. Dr. McQuay was especially interested in equipping his students to minister to parents having to deal with the loss of a child. As part of the class, he read aloud the heart-tugging testimony of a father whose son, a strapping young man, had died following heart surgery.

After class, Dr. McQuay proceeded to the college dining room and was just about to take his first bite of lunch when a secretary appeared by his side. "Dr. McQuay," she said, "you have an emergency phone call from North Carolina." McQuay's heart skipped a beat; his own son, Tim, a newly married medical student, was in North Carolina.

The news was tragic. While adjusting his car's sound system, Tim had lost control of the vehicle. The crash was severe, and Tim was not expected to survive.

Dr. and Mrs. McQuay immediately rushed to North Carolina. That night in the hospital chapel, they knelt in great pain and with many tears. Lifting their hands to God, they prayed, "Lord, when Tim was a baby we held him up to You and gave him to You. And we have maintained that commitment through the twenty-three years of his life. Again now we lift him to You. You are our sovereign Lord, and Your plan is perfect."

Tragically, Tim passed away.

Looking back, nothing could have prepared the McQuays for the ensuing grief and anguish. Dr. McQuay later wrote, "The theological side of me declares, 'Tim is alive in heaven and all is well. Rejoice!' But there is a humanly frail side of me that cries, 'My dear son is gone. And I miss him so!' I know that separation is only temporary. Yet I hurt deeply. My strength fails. Dark clouds hide the sun. I feel alone. My heart cries for my son."[1]

Watching our loved ones suffer or try to find their way through trouble may be one of the most difficult things we can endure. We want so desperately to help! We want to make

"My dear son is gone.
And I miss him so!"

things easier. We want to make things right—and we sometimes have difficulty understanding why God doesn't step in to do just that.

Like the McQuays, most God-fearing parents experience conflicting emotions when it comes to challenges affecting our families, and especially our children. On the one hand, we understand intellectually that the best thing we can do for our family members is release them to God—release them to follow His plan and encounter His will in whatever ways are necessary. That's true even when it means allowing our family members to experience painful circumstances that lead to critical lessons learned.

On the other hand, that is easier said than done.

Perhaps the only thing worse than pondering whether God has forgotten us is the idea that God has forgotten those in our family.

I'd like to offer three ways you can respond in such moments. You can replace your fear with faith, your sorrow with God's Word, and your heartache with trust.

REPLACE FEAR WITH FAITH

The story of Jairus's daughter documents one of the most memorable teaching moments in the Gospels. Not because of the outcome—yes, a miracle happened when a young girl was raised from the dead, but that is not surprising given the overall context of Jesus' life and ministry. Instead, the remarkable moment came in the form of an interruption that must have been disturbing if you look at the story from Jairus's point of view—it taught him to replace fear with faith.

At the time, Jesus was teaching near a synagogue in Galilee when a man named Jairus approached Him. Jairus was the leader of the synagogue, which meant he was part of the religious elite that often opposed Jesus. This time, however, Jairus fell at Jesus' feet and "begged Him to come to his house, for he had an only daughter about twelve years of age, and she was dying" (Luke 8:41–42).

Jesus agreed to go with this man, and they set off through the crowd.

While on the way to Jairus's house, another event occurred. A woman who had suffered from "a flow of blood" for twelve years approached Jesus through the crowd and stealthily touched His robe (v. 43). This was significant because the woman's condition likely meant she had been ritually unclean for all of those twelve years—unable to attend worship or make sacrifices at the temple, and unable even to touch other people. By touching Jesus, she was taking an incredible risk.

You've likely heard or read the rest of her story:

Jesus said, "Who touched Me?"

When all denied it, Peter and those with Him said, "Master, the multitudes throng and press You, and You say, 'Who touched Me?'"

But Jesus said, "Somebody touched Me, for I perceived power going out from Me." Now when the woman saw that she was not hidden, she came trembling; and falling down before Him, she declared to Him in the presence of all the people the reason she had touched Him and how she was healed immediately.

And He said to her, "Daughter, be of good cheer; your faith has made you well. Go in peace." (vv. 45–48)

All this was great news for the unnamed woman, and the incident revealed both Jesus' power and His compassion.

But what about Jairus? Try to replay those events from his point of view. Would you be pleased if your daughter was on the point of death, you had finally convinced the one Person who could help to come and see her—and then someone else jumped in front of you with their problems and their concerns? Would you wait patiently while Jesus asked His questions, chatted with Peter, and then continued to engage with this unknown woman? This woman who had just broken many of the social and religious rules of her culture?

For Jairus, it must have

seemed like Jesus had forgotten

all about his little girl.

For Jairus, it must have seemed like Jesus had forgotten all about his little girl.

And then everything got much, much worse: "While He was still speaking, someone came from the ruler of the synagogue's house, saying to him, 'Your daughter is dead. Do not trouble the Teacher'" (v. 49).

Of course, Jesus had not forgotten about Jairus's daughter. He knew exactly what was happening in those moments. More importantly, He knew exactly what was going to happen. That's why He gave Jairus these instructions: "Do not be afraid; only believe, and she will be made well" (v. 50).

Those words apply to anyone who wonders whether God has forgotten about their family members. *Do not be afraid. Only believe.*

The reality is plain and simple: If you could solve the problems your loved ones are facing, you would have done so by now. If those same loved ones were able to navigate themselves through life without experiencing any pain or difficulty, they would certainly do it. Therefore, there comes a time when "doing" is no longer helpful and when fear exacerbates our anxiety.

In such moments, faith is the answer. Belief in God's goodness and care is not simply an option—it is the *only* option that can produce any good. Make the choice of intentionally replacing your fear with faith.

REPLACE SORROW WITH GOD'S WORD

Sadly, there are times when God's good and perfect will does not include healing on earth for those we love. Instead, their healing comes in heaven—which means there are times when we lose the very people we are sure we could never live without. Because of that reality, I want to offer a special note to parents who have endured the death of a child.

Sometime after his son's death, Dr. Earl McQuay wrote a small book titled *Beyond Eagles: A Father's Grief and Hope* in which he listed five realities that provided immense comfort to his heart and to his wife's. I offer a summary of those realities in the hopes that they will be a road map to comfort for those who long to find it.

The first reality is Scripture. The infallible Word of God served as firm ground on which Dr. McQuay and his wife could withstand the hurricane of tragedy that swept over their souls. They found verses, claimed promises, studied truths about heaven, and drew near to the Lord day by day within the covers of His Book.

The second is prayer. Through prayer, they could cry out before the throne of God, knowing He sympathized with their weaknesses. They also felt the support of many others who were praying for them. In prayer we are able to rest in God's arms, find comfort in His presence, pour out our hearts to Him, and trust Him to turn our heartaches into memories—and ultimately into praise.

The third is friends. "At the time of our greatest need," wrote McQuay, "the members of the body of Christ came to our relief. Their many cards, letters, flowers, food, memorial gifts, calls and prayers encouraged us and aided the healing process."

The fourth is memories. Dr. McQuay and his wife relished the twenty-three years they had enjoyed with Tim. Nothing could take away those smiles, laughs, and good times.

Finally, hope. For the Christian, death is not a period but a comma in the story—only a pause; and all our separations are temporary. Christians part only to meet again.[2]

My words can never reduce a parent's pain, but I believe with all my heart that God's Word can impart eternal comfort. He who said, "Let the little children come to Me" (Mark 10:14) is preparing an everlasting city where friendships will never end, relationships will never sour, separations will never divide, and death will never intrude.

Our time on earth is but a moment, and then we're gone. But our God is from everlasting to everlasting, and He has prepared a place for us. Let's comfort one another with His Word.

For the Christian, death is not a period but a comma in the story.

REPLACE YOUR HEARTACHE
WITH TRUST

Of course, the relationships within a family involve more than parents and their children. The connection between the husband and wife can be the source of the greatest joy or the most intense pain in a person's life.

Just as with our children, when our spouse is going through a difficult time, or even a season of suffering, our heart breaks along with theirs. When our partner in life is in trouble and we can't do anything to solve the issue, it understandably causes us pain.

But there's another aspect to events causing disruption in the home—sometimes the heartache comes from the actions of our spouse. They may be making poor health or financial decisions, which causes strife. Or perhaps they are sharp or cruel with their tongue, signaling that their spiritual life and connection with God are not where they should be.

Or perhaps a disconnection in the home caused the marriage to completely disintegrate. Separation and divorce have been rampant in our society for decades—yes, even in the church—and our families are often forced to suffer the consequences.

What can we do when our familial relationships are in disarray?

Ephesians 5 is often referenced as the "marriage chapter"

within Scripture. That's largely because these verses offer powerful and practical application for our deepest relationships. For example, in verses 22–28, Paul instructs wives to show the same respect to their husbands that they show to God. If that sounds like a tall order, Paul instructs husbands to love their wives with the same self-sacrificial love Christ demonstrated when He offered Himself as a living sacrifice for the Church!

One way to summarize Paul's instruction to husbands and wives is this: Take responsibility for your role in your relationship by putting Christ as the priority—both in your actions and words—and then trust God with the outcome.

It's easy to focus on what you'd like to be different in your marriage. Unfortunately, it's also easy to drift into a lifestyle of attempting to change your spouse. Sometimes that happens vocally through nagging or criticism, and other times it happens through silence and emotional manipulation. Many spouses become active in striving to "fix" the one they love.

What we need to understand is that we don't have control over our spouse. We can't control their thoughts. We can't control their desires. We can't control their behavior or habits or goals or spirituality.

But we do have control over ourselves! We can control our own thoughts, desires, behavior, habits, goals, and spiritual lives.

What we need to understand is that we don't have control over our spouse.

We can change and improve who we are and how we relate to our spouse—approaching each other with love, respect, and an ongoing sacrificial commitment to the marriage.

The added benefit of choosing to "fix" ourselves rather than our spouse is that it allows room for trust. Specifically, as we learn to trust God to work in the lives of those we love most, our faith grows as He works to restore broken or fragmented relationships.

God has not forgotten your family. In reality, nobody loves your family more than He does. Nobody is rooting for your family more than God. And nobody but God has the means and the power and the authority and the wisdom to guide each member of your family to where they need to go.

Therefore, take a step back and choose to trust God.

Six

GOD HAS NOT FORGOTTEN YOU WHEN YOU ARE LONELY

Recently a young, single woman quit her job in the city and moved back to her small hometown, abandoning her career and leaving a place of service in the church she had joined. When asked why she made the move, she replied, "I just got tired of eating alone." No one is immune from loneliness. Even one of the most brilliant men who ever lived, Albert Einstein, complained, "It is strange to be known so universally, and yet to be so lonely."

Loneliness is not new—it has been present throughout history. Today is no exception; in fact, loneliness reaches beyond borders and economic status—affecting both the young and old. Spouses are lonely. Singles are lonely. Seniors are lonely. Soldiers are lonely. Students are

Sometimes it seems as if no one, not even God, cares about us.

lonely. The list seems endless. The recent restrictions placed on us due to the pandemic have kept people from interacting with others in person, creating a problem with isolation and loneliness that was unknown previously. God created us to have interaction with one another *and* with Him. The truth is, God never leaves us alone, not for a moment. Yet sometimes we feel alone. Sometimes it seems as if no one, not even God, cares about us.

It is in those moments when the body of Christ needs to reach out and be the hands and feet of our Savior. Even with restrictions on how and when we get to see one another in person, it should be our priority to seek those who are hurting and make contact with them in some way to let them know someone cares—a note, a phone call, an email—the opportunities are there if we will look for them. D. L. Moody said it this way: "The world does not understand theology or dogma, but it understands love and sympathy."[1] This is especially true during a time of loss, which many people are experiencing in recent days. Perhaps the loneliest people on earth are survivors, those who live on after a loved one has died.

THE LONELINESS OF LOSING SOMEONE

North Carolina evangelist Vance Havner possessed a sharp mind and a dry wit that made his one-liners legendary. He had a unique way of turning a phrase so that it tickled your ribs and pierced your heart, both at once.

But Havner's most popular and powerful book wasn't a volume of sermons or a collection of devotions. It was an account of his own personal anguish over losing his wife to a dreaded and fatal disease. Out of the crucible of suffering, he wrote *Though I Walk Through the Valley*, a book that contains no pat answers or time-worn clichés.

"Sara is gone," Havner wrote. "Gone with her are a thousand other precious things that made the past years so delightful. Gone the anticipation of returning home to be greeted at the airport or the apartment door. Gone the thrill of hearing that voice at the other end of the telephone. . . . Gone those airmail letters in the motel box, one every day. Gone the clasp of that dear hand as we strolled about all over the country. Gone that lovely face in the congregation, smiling at my jokes she had heard countless times before."[2]

Gone. Just like *loss*, it's a four-letter word, cruel in its effect but unavoidable for pilgrims trudging through a world not their own.

When a spouse dies, our world changes. Our daily routine changes. Our sleeping habits change. Our appetite and enjoyment of life are affected, and intense pain and loneliness come and go with no predictable patterns. There's no feeling as lonely as listening for a voice that no longer speaks or waiting for the touch of a vanished hand.

Gone. Just like loss, it's a four-letter word, cruel in its effect but unavoidable for pilgrims trudging through a world not their own.

Yet there is hope. Because even when you enter the loneliest valley imaginable, God is still with you. Even when it feels like your heart has been ripped in two, God has not forgotten you. His voice is still there. His touch is still real. And His care is unmeasured.

Throughout Scripture God shows His concern for the lonely as He calls on us to care for widows and widowers in their distress. Widows are mentioned frequently in the law of Moses, especially in Deuteronomy. The Old Testament laws contained multiple provisions and protections for those whose spouses had died. Israel's justice system was particularly keen to the rights and needs of widows.

In fact, one entire book in the Bible is devoted to the plight of two different women whose husbands had died: Naomi and Ruth. When Naomi lost both her husband and her sons while living in a foreign land, she planned to return to Israel alone in loneliness and grief. Yet Ruth, Naomi's daughter-in-law and herself a grieving widow, would not allow it. She joined Naomi on that journey, and the two women chose to support and encourage each other when all other consolation seemed far away. What gives this story special meaning is that Ruth is the great-grandmother of King David—and a distant ancestor of Jesus Himself. Meaning, God's remarkable care and guidance over the lives of these two women set the stage for the subsequent redemptive history of Israel.

One of the most unusual and instructive stories of the Old

Testament concerns Elijah and the widow of Zarephath. During a time of famine, this widow's pantry was nearly empty, yet she shared what she had with Elijah. As a result, her bin of flour "was not used up, nor did the jar of oil run dry" (1 Kings 17:16). The stories of Elijah, Elisha, and the widows they met provide lessons about how God cares for those who have lost a loved one and how He wants to use them as a blessing to others.

Isaiah 54:5, which is sometimes called the "widow's verse," has bestowed infinite comfort to generations of grieving women: "For your Maker is your husband, the LORD of hosts is His name." For fifty years Agnes and her husband Emit had morning Bible reading and prayer at the breakfast table. On the day he died, she went to bed thinking that she could never again start the day with devotional exercises. But the next morning she bravely sat at the kitchen table and opened her Bible to the spot where she and her husband had quit their reading twenty-four hours before. The verse that stared up at her was Isaiah 54:5—*For your Maker is your husband.*

She smiled and said, "Thank You, Lord." Through those words in Isaiah, God comforted Agnes in that extreme moment of loss and loneliness.

In the New Testament, the Lord Jesus had many encounters with widows. During the first days of His life, He was blessed by the prophetess Anna, a widow of eighty-four years; and during the last moments of His life He made sure that His own widowed mother was provided for by the apostle John (John 19:16–27). In between these two widows were many others, including the famous widow who, in her poverty, placed her mite in the temple treasure and was commended by our Lord for her faithful generosity (Luke 21:1–4).

What does all this mean for you? First, that in times of great loss, we can be comforted by God's care for those most vulnerable to loneliness and despair. If you find yourself grieving the loss of someone you never planned to live without, you can trust that God will find ways to demonstrate His care for you.

Second, you can find comfort in the simple truth that you are never alone. Yes, death can cause us pain, but Jesus removed the sting of death for the believer. He won the victory over death! Christ conquered the grave, which means He offers a balm to our grieving hearts. Life on this side of eternity is filled with partings, but we don't have to experience those partings alone. We have the comforting presence of His Spirit with us now and the enduring hope of eternal life with Christ one day in heaven.

THE REALITY OF REJECTION

Rejection is another major factor in the lives of those struggling with loneliness. All too often, it's not the passing of a loved one

If you find yourself grieving the loss of someone you never planned to live without, you can trust that God will find ways to demonstrate His care for you.

that causes our pain but the judgment and denunciation of one who once cared about us.

Family rejection is the worst kind of hurt. Whether it's a spouse who stops loving you, a dad who walks out of your life, a mother who wants nothing more to do with you, a sibling from whom you are estranged, or a child who leaves home in anger or prodigality—the disconnect from someone you love is always a devastating loss.

Divorce is often understood as more painful than the death of a spouse because it involves a choice. Somewhere within that divorce, there's usually a level of rejection not seen when a loved one passes away.

The love and support of one's family is the basis of self-worth, mental health, goal setting, and the ability to interact positively with others. The benefits of receiving affirmation are endless. When we lose the support and praise of those we love the most, the pain is tremendous.

Once again, the Bible is not silent on this subject. Instead, its pages are filled with the consequences of rejection in many forms.

For example, the first death in history occurred when Cain and Abel had a falling out. Later in Genesis, the same story is echoed in the rejection of Joseph by his brothers. Many years later, the remorseful brothers were still haunted by their betrayal of Joseph, saying to one another, "We are truly guilty . . . for we saw the

When we lose the support and
praise of those we love the most,
the pain is tremendous.

anguish in his soul when he pleaded with us, and we would not hear; therefore this distress has come upon us" (Genesis 42:21).

We discussed the story of Job in a previous chapter, yet one of his greatest sorrows was the loss of his children followed by the loss of support from his wife, as recorded in chapters 1–2. You may remember her only line in the book: "Do you still hold fast to your integrity? Curse God and die!" (2:9).

In the life of Jesus, there were several occasions when His family withdrew their understanding and support. John 7:5 says, "For even His brothers did not believe in Him." In Mark 3, they feared He was "out of His mind" (v. 21). Perhaps even more crushing was the total collapse of our Lord's circle of support on the night He was arrested. Judas betrayed Him, Peter denied Him, and all His disciples fled, leaving Him alone. On the cross, even the Heavenly Father turned His back, leading Jesus to cry, "My God, My God, why have You forsaken Me?" (Matthew 27:46).

Our feelings of loss are especially acute if our family resents us because of our faith in Christ. Francis Schaeffer understood what this felt like. Today we remember him as a Christian missionary apologist who challenged a world of skeptics to consider the truths of the Bible. But as a young man, Francis faced hostile parents who fiercely opposed his idea of going into the ministry. They'd always wanted their son to be an engineer. In preparing for Christian service, he went against their wishes so that his mother carried an unforgiving and bitter spirit far into his years of ministry and into old age.

How can we respond in such moments? Here are four ways you can turn to God during seasons of loneliness and rejection— because no matter what others may choose, God will never forget or forsake you.

A FATHER WHO LOVES US

If you're feeling a level of rejection today, remember you still have a Heavenly Father who loves you. Because Christ was forsaken by God, we need never be. Because He was separated from His Father's love on Calvary, we are united in the Father's love forever. The apostle Paul prayed that his readers would comprehend "what is the width and length and depth and height" of God's love for us (Ephesians 3:18).

Romans 8 says that nothing in all of creation can separate us from His love (vv. 38–39). Colossians 3 says that our lives are hidden with Christ in God (v. 3). John 10 says that nothing can ever snatch us out of His hand (v. 28). "When my father and my mother forsake me," says Psalm 27:10, "then the LORD will take care of me."

In Isaiah 49:15–16, the Lord said, "Can a woman forget her

nursing child, and not have compassion on the son of her womb? Surely they may forget, yet I will not forget you. See, I have inscribed you on the palms of My hands."

Faced with His friends deserting Him on the eve of His crucifixion, Jesus said, "Indeed the hour is coming, yes, has now come, that you will be scattered, each to his own, and will leave Me alone. And yet I am not alone, because the Father is with Me" (John 16:32). It was the Father's presence that strengthened Jesus during His arrest and trial, and feeling the loss of the Father's presence on the cross proved His greatest anguish. But His anguish became our answer.

Echoing the words of Jesus, the apostle Paul said in his last surviving paragraph, just prior to his own execution, "At my first defense no one stood with me, but all forsook me. . . . But the Lord stood with me and strengthened me" (2 Timothy 4:16–17).

Our Father has repeatedly promised never to leave us or forsake us. If we could only understand the depth of God's love for us, much of our loneliness would be relieved.

A BROTHER WHO DIED FOR US

We also have a Brother who died for us. Think of how grateful we should be for our kinship with Jesus Christ. He called us His friends and His brothers, and He said in John 15:13–14, "Greater love has no one than this, than to lay down one's life for his friends. You are My friends."

When Christiana Tsai, the daughter of a Chinese political leader, announced to her family she had become a Christian, she was engulfed in successive waves of abuse, ridicule, rejection, and persecution. One of her brothers tore up her Bible in front of her. But Christiana later wrote, "I . . . silently looked to God. Suddenly I saw a vision of Christ on the cross, a crown of thorns on His head and with nails in His hands, and I knew He had suffered for my sins, had purchased my head with His crown, and my hands with His nails. Was there anything I couldn't bear for Him who had suffered so much for me?"

Christiana determined to treat her family as graciously as possible, knowing that Christ was beside her, loving and strengthening her. Later one of her older brothers came to her. "Tell me about Christianity and why you became a Christian," he asked, adding, "I have noticed that in spite of the way we treat you now, you seem much happier than you used to be. I think I would like to believe, too."[3]

When we lean on the strength of our elder Brother, walking in His steps, resting in His love, and devoted to His cause, we'll find that He can actively work in painful situations, and He can give us a gracious spirit. Any form of rejection or loneliness—even including the loss of family support—can be turned to gain as He works all things together for our good (Romans 8:28).

A COMFORTER WHO WALKS WITH US

We have a third pillar of support: a Comforter who walks with us. In the Upper Room Discourse of John 13–17, Jesus told His disciples that though He was leaving them, He was not abandoning them. "It is to your advantage that I go away," He said in John 16:7.

That's a remarkable statement—it's to our *advantage* that Jesus leave us, leave the world? It's *better* for us that He's gone?

Yes, Jesus said. "It is to your advantage that I go away; for if I do not go away, the Helper [Comforter] will not come to you; but if I depart, I will send Him to you."

That's our ultimate reservoir of grace. It's the Holy Spirit of Christ who lives within us, through whom our Lord lives in our heart, mind, and very body. It's the Holy Spirit who fills us with boldness to speak the Word. It's the Holy Spirit who produces the fruit of the Spirit—love, joy, peace, patience, kindness, goodness, faithfulness, gentleness, and self-control. It's the Holy Spirit who brings to mind the Word of God and helps us recall promises at critical moments. It's the Holy Spirit who illumines our minds as we study the Bible so that God's Word burns within our hearts. And it's the Holy Spirit who ministers to our spirits, reassuring us that we are God's children.

None of this is lost when we experience loneliness or rejection. In fact, in those moments the Comforter becomes even dearer and His comfort even more precious.

A FAMILY WHO BELONGS TO US

Finally, we have a family who belongs to us, and to whom we belong: the Church. The fellowship of Christians is the body of Christ and the family of God. When Jesus felt rejected by kin, He said that His real brothers and sisters were "whoever does the will of God" (Mark 3:35). He had more affinity with His followers who believed in Him than with His own family who didn't.

In a similar way, sometimes we find our greatest support, love, friendship, and fellowship with God's people in our Christian friendships, small groups, and church gatherings.

Whenever we feel lonely or rejected, we must guard against withdrawing into isolationism. We can't become recluses, rejecting the world and everyone in it. Even lovers of solitude need to reach out in love, finding someone to serve, seeking a kindness to do during these challenging times.

So let me say it again: There is hope during the most challenging seasons of life. Even in the most painful of rejections. That's because we have a Savior who is the God of hope. When we have the love of a Father, the support of a Brother, the presence of a Comforter, and the availability of the family of God, there's more than hope.

There's victory.

Seven

GOD HAS NOT FORGOTTEN
YOU WHEN HEALTH FAILS

Human health, and the human body in general, is a paradox.

In many ways your body is incredibly robust and powerful—even miraculously so. Your immune system is a finely calibrated force of assassins and counter-intelligence personnel so efficient that it routinely eliminates all manner of threats to your well-being, from bacteria to viruses to rogue cancer cells and more. Even when something goes wrong, your body is amazingly adaptive at healing itself.

When you skin a knee or receive a deep cut, for example, little cells in your bloodstream called platelets immediately detect the breach and set out to make things right. They join together in a matrix or network that quickly coagulates and seals off any affected blood vessels to prevent further bleeding. Then, seemingly overnight in most cases, new skin grows in the place of what was damaged. I've seen my grandchildren marvel at the way their bodies heal after an injury.

And we should marvel! Our bodies function as living, breathing pictures of God's goodness and care.

Yet in other ways, our bodies can seem incredibly frail and prone to failure. We feel this more keenly the older we get.

To give you an example of that frailty, what do you think is the most dangerous animal on planet Earth? Which creature would you guess is most harmful to humans?

If your first thought is of animals with sharp teeth and claws such as sharks or bears, you're in the wrong ballpark. Sharks kill only a few dozen people each year. Larger mammals kill fewer than that. What about snakes? They certainly are deadly, and their venom is responsible for tens of thousands of human deaths each year. But there is a far greater killer lurking in the shadows.

Incredibly, the creature most dangerous to human beings is the mosquito. That's because mosquitoes are responsible for the transmission of diseases such as malaria, yellow fever, dengue fever, Zika, and more—diseases that collectively kill more than 750,000 people every year.[1]

As a pastor who has visited many hospital beds, and as someone who has found myself in the grip of severe illness in the past, I understand how demoralizing it can feel when our own bodies fail us—when the health and strength we've always relied on is no longer there. In such moments, it's easy to become swallowed up by fear and doubt. *Does God understand what I am going through here? Does He care? Has He forgotten about me?*

What are Christians to make of the ever-present reality of disease? How are we to live knowing that our lives could be disrupted at any moment—indeed, could be ended—by something we can't even see?

THE SOURCE OF SICKNESS

Disease is nothing more or less than a symptom of sin. Not personal sin, but the curse of sin on all creation (Genesis 3:17–19). As the apostle Paul wrote in Romans 8:18–25, all creation labors under the burden of sin and longs for the day of redemption when there will be no more "death, nor sorrow, nor crying. . . . No more pain" (Revelation 21:4).

Until that day, we live in the same way we were saved: by the grace of God.

God created Adam and Eve in a state of perfect health, and their bodies were free from disease. When they sinned, the whole order of nature convulsed; sickness became a grim reality, and death an unavoidable eventuality.

All of us will experience illness, injury, incapacity, and ultimately death during our time here on earth. The loss of health may come suddenly or slowly. But through it all, God does not give us a spirit of fear, but of power, of love, and of a sound mind. We can't give in to panic or allow ourselves to live in a state of depression or fear, for the joy of the Lord remains our strength in every situation.

It helps us remember that even the biblical heroes of old weren't immunized against illness. Job suffered prolonged illnesses that marred his body and brought constant misery. Paul watched helplessly as his friends Epaphroditus and Trophimus tossed and turned with deadly fever. Hezekiah was struck by terminal illness, and King Asa had a wasting disease in his feet. Peter's mother-in-law occupied a sickbed, Samuel became feeble, and King David anguished over the condition of his newborn. Paul prayed three times to be healed of his illness, the thorn in his flesh. And even the Son of Man suffered violent, life-ending injuries and excruciating pain at the hands of His enemies.

THE SOLUTION TO SICKNESS

Even in illness and injury, we need to be biblical Christians, claiming God's promises and living with His presence and purposes in mind. We need to live in faith, not fear.

With that being said, here are four specific steps you can take when sickness or the loss of health makes it seem as if God has forgotten you.

Keep Trusting God

Our greatest challenge in the loss of health is to keep trusting God. We know He cares for us, and we know we have ultimate healing through the shed blood and empty tomb of Jesus Christ. But the loss of health affects us emotionally as much as physically. It puts us at risk financially and vocationally. It sets us on a collision course with our most dreaded enemy—death—and we may find ourselves in real mortal danger, exposed to possible suffering, chronic pain, and the loss of all we hold dear in life.

Perhaps the greatest truth in the entire Bible as it relates to sickness among Christians is John 11:4 when Jesus declared, "This sickness will not end in death. No, it is for God's glory so that God's Son may be glorified through it" (NIV).

Christ spoke those words after hearing that His friend, Lazarus, was ill. Lazarus was indeed sick, and he *did* die. By the time Jesus arrived, he'd been in the tomb for four days. But Jesus didn't say that Lazarus's sickness wouldn't *include* death. He said it wouldn't *end* in death. It would provide instead an occasion for God to be glorified.

Do you know the term "10–4"? It's part of the "ten codes"

used by police officers to communicate quickly over radio. To say "10–4" is to signal that you understand and agree.

Well, Christians who are experiencing sickness shouldn't say "10–4" but "11:4," and I recommend John 11:4 be inscribed in the hospital suite or the sickroom of every believer in the world today. Why? Because our illness will not end in death. Instead, everything that happens to us will become a platform for the glory of Him who "works all things according to the counsel of His will" (Ephesians 1:11).

Therefore, we can continue to trust God even in the grip of illness and pain.

Work to Stay Spiritually Strong

I want to avoid giving the impression that dealing with sickness should be simple or easy—because it's not. The answer in times of physical distress is rarely praying for a few moments each day, trusting that God will take care of everything, and then going about our regular lives. Sickness is more complicated. *Life* is more complicated.

For these reasons, we have to work hard at staying spiritually and emotionally strong during illness. At times we need physical therapy, but God is a great spiritual therapist who can help keep us strong of heart even when we're weak of body. Proverbs 18:14 says, "The spirit of a man will sustain him in sickness."

In earlier times, Christian publishers commissioned hymn-books specifically geared for the sick and disabled to help foster this attitude. The great hymnist J. M. Neale, for example, edited a nineteenth-century volume titled *The Invalid's Hymn-Book: Being a Selection of Hymns Appropriate to the Sick-Room*. It aimed to bolster the spiritual and emotional health of those whose physical health was in decline.

One such hymn in Neale's book said,

> *Are thy toils and woes increasing?*
> *Are the foe's attacks unceasing?*
> *Look with Faith unclouded,*
> *Gaze with eyes unshrouded,*
> *On the Cross!*[2]

The apostle Paul spoke along these lines when he said, "Therefore we do not lose heart. Even though our outward man is perishing, yet the inward man is being renewed day by day" (2 Corinthians 4:16).

Periods of illness can be times in which we discover new realms of the faithfulness of God, which is why the Victorian preacher Charles H. Spurgeon once declared, "I dare say that the greatest earthly blessing that God can give to any of us is health, with the exception of sickness."[3]

Seek to Be Useful

We also have to remember that as long as we're in this world, God intends to use us. Our work isn't over until He takes us home. The prophet Elisha was still counseling kings in his sickness that would end in his death (2 Kings 13:14). A glance at Christian history tells us that some of the greatest works for God have been done by people battling sickness, disease, or disability.

We have to persevere as best we can, aiming to do the work God has for us each day. "You can't get much done in life if you only work when you feel good," said basketball star Jerry West.

John Pounds is a good example. He was a tall, muscular teenaged laborer at the docks of Portsmouth, England, who slipped and fell from the top of a ship's mast. When workers reached him, he was nothing but a mass of broken bones. For two years he lay in bed as his bones healed crookedly. His pain never ceased. Out of boredom, he began to read the Bible.

At length, John crawled from bed hoping to find something he could do with his life. A shoemaker eventually hired him. Day after day, John sat at his cobbler's bench, a Bible open on his lap. Soon he came to faith in Christ and was born again.

John ultimately gathered enough money to purchase his own little shoe shop, and one day he developed a pair of surgical boots for his crippled nephew Johnny, whom he had taken

"You can't get much done in life if
you only work when you feel good."

in. Soon John was making corrective shoes for other children, and his little cobbler's shop became a miniature children's hospital.

As John's burden for children grew, he began receiving homeless children, feeding them, teaching them to read, and telling them about the Lord. His shop became known as "The Ragged School," and John would limp around the waterfront, food in his pockets, looking for more children to tend.

During his lifetime, John Pounds rescued five hundred children from despair. Incredibly, he led every one of them to Christ. Moreover, his work became so famous that a "Ragged School Movement" swept England, and a series of laws were passed to establish schools for poor children in John's honor. Boys' homes, girls' homes, day schools, and evening schools were started, along with Bible classes in which thousands heard the Gospel.

After John collapsed and died on New Year's Day 1839, while tending to a boy's ulcerated foot, he was buried in a churchyard on High Street. All England mourned, and a monument was erected over his grave, reading, "Thou shalt be blessed, for they could not recompense thee."[4]

John Pounds is a good reminder that God isn't finished with us just because we grow frail or feeble. So seek out opportunities to be useful in His kingdom as long as there is still light in your eyes and breath in your lungs.

Stay Focused on Heaven

Finally, Christians are practical people who understand that eventually we're going to make it to heaven, and it will be via the valley of the shadow of death. We may not relish the thought of death, but we're not worried. We recall that Jesus interrupted every funeral He attended, and He delighted in healing the sick.

Indeed, every story of healing in the Bible is a token of God's ultimate, eternal healing of all our bodily afflictions, which is part of our redemption through Christ, by whose stripes we are healed.

An old Puritan once said, "Sickness, when sanctified, teaches us four things: The vanity of the world, the vileness of sin, the helplessness of man and the preciousness of Christ."

If heaven is the worst thing that can happen to us, we shouldn't despair even amid medical emergencies or the loss of health. We have a Great Physician whose own tomb is empty. We have a heavenly home whose doors are open. And we have a sympathetic Savior who never imparts a spirit of fear, but of power, love, and a sound mind (2 Timothy 1:7).

Eight

GOD HAS NOT FORGOTTEN YOU WHEN PRAYERS GO UNANSWERED

We live in a day where everything seems to happen faster all the time—including shipping and package delivery. It wasn't that long ago that receiving a package three days after placing an order was considered "expedited" shipping. Then Amazon came along and revolutionized our expectations with free two-day shipping as part of their "Prime" service. Now, it's not a problem to get same-day delivery on many items if you live in the right place.

All of that explains why Elliot Berinstein's recent experiences are so surprising.

A doctor in the city of Toronto, Canada, Berinstein was surprised to see a package on his porch when he arrived home after work one day. He didn't remember ordering anything, and he certainly didn't remember any purchases from the sender, Well. ca, which is a Canadian health and beauty website.

That was May 6, 2020.

Opening the package, Berinstein found a tube of Brylcreem hair product, which stirred something in his memory. Then he checked the invoice and solved the mystery. The package had originally been fulfilled and mailed through Canada Post on August 1, 2012.

His delivery had taken eight years to arrive!

Berinstein has no explanation for the extreme delay. "I think it was just in a corner somewhere and then someone just decided to mail it," he said. "I thought it was pretty funny that they just didn't throw it out or something. . . . I wonder why they sent it out now since they're pretty far behind on their current packages and stuff."[1]

That's a positive attitude for an eight-year delay. Most of us get irritated when an email takes too long to arrive, let alone a physical package. We like it best when people and companies follow our preferred timelines without any unnecessary waiting.

As Christians, we face similar frustrations when God refuses to follow our timeline in terms of answering our prayers. Indeed, there are few experiences that cause us to question God's care more than when we bow before Him in prayer, reach out in genuine faith, make our sincere requests known to God, and then we hear—nothing. No answer. No guidance. No response whatsoever.

At least not right away.

Obviously, we like it when God responds to our prayers by saying, "Yes." It's always a blessing to receive an answer from our Heavenly Father. Even when God answers our prayers with "No," we can find peace. We can trust that He knows best and move on.

However, there are other times when God delays answering our prayers for reasons known only to Him. When we receive neither a yes nor a no, we are forced to endure our current circumstances as we wait for God's response to finally come.

David has given us a good example to follow in such moments.

OUR STRUGGLE WHEN GOD DELAYS

In chapter 1, we explored the circumstances that caused David to write Psalm 13. He had been anointed the future king of Israel as a young man and had achieved national fame by slaying the giant Goliath. But then David spent years languishing in the wilderness as he tried to outwit and outmaneuver Saul and his armies, all the while waiting for God to fulfill His promise.

Even when God answers our prayers with "No," we can find peace. We can trust that He knows best and move on.

In other words, Psalm 13 was born out of a moment when David felt deeply frustrated with God's delay. No wonder the first two words of the psalm are "How long?"

Aren't you grateful for psalms that reveal the deepest thoughts of the writer? God knows what we're going through, so He is not surprised by our entreaties. He is ready to listen to our prayers in our time of trouble—just as He did for David.

So, let's explore together three ways David's psalm reflects our feelings when God delays answering our prayers.

We Feel Forgotten

"How long, O LORD?" David cried out. "Will You forget me forever?" (v. 1).

As we've seen throughout this book, David's question is common for followers of God. We all go through it at one time or another—feeling that God isn't there or at the very least that He has forgotten us. Perhaps we even wonder at times if our problems are important to Him.

Another psalmist encountered those very doubts in Psalm 10:1 when he wrote, "Why do You stand afar off, O LORD? Why do You hide in times of trouble?"

You see, everyone has a point somewhere in the geography of their souls marking the limits of their faith. It is the point at which faith begins to unravel. Only we know where the point lies, and we often discover it during a season of testing. A trial builds to a crescendo in your life. You attempt to handle it; you pray about it. But life does not cooperate. And as the days turn to weeks, and then weeks to months, and months even to years, you reach that personal point, somewhere in the scheme of your suffering, when you begin to give up on God.

What you really believe is that God has given up on you. You may even be feeling that way right now. If so, please allow me to remind you that what you're contemplating is a simple impossibility. God never gives up on you, He never ceases to care about you, and He will not abandon you—even during your trial. I'm reminded again of the poignant words in Isaiah 49:15–16: "Can a woman forget her nursing child, and not have compassion on the son of her womb? Surely they may forget, yet I will not forget you. See, I have inscribed you on the palms of My hands; your walls are continually before Me."

Such is God's concern for you. He cannot forget you. No matter what storm you're weathering now, you have never left God's mind or His heart.

We Feel Forsaken

Yes, sometimes when God delays, we feel forgotten. But it can get even worse. Sometimes when God delays, we feel forsaken. Read on in Psalm 13:1: "How long will you hide your face from me?" (NIV).

God never gives up on you, He never
ceases to care about you, and He will
not abandon you—even during your trial.

Now, *forgotten* is one thing, but *forsaken* is another matter entirely. We very innocently forget people at times, even people we love and care about. That can happen in the hectic pace of life. But the act of forsaking is very intentional. It is *premeditated forgetfulness.*

That's how David felt in this moment, and I know that is how you have felt as well: *My God, why have You forsaken me?*

You might recognize those words. Jesus said them in His anguish on the cross. Do you know where Jesus got those words? He quoted them from Psalm 22, which was also written by David: "My God, My God, why have You forsaken Me? Why are You so far from helping Me, and from the words of My groaning? O My God, I cry in the daytime, but You do not hear; and in the night season, and am not silent" (vv. 1–2).

It's helpful to know that David suffered and felt forsaken. But it's life changing to realize that even Jesus Himself, the Lord of heaven and earth enclosed in flesh, experienced the same emotions. Imagine! The Lord Jesus Christ not only felt forsaken, *He was forsaken.* God turned His back on Jesus because He is a holy and just God who would not look on the sin Jesus carried to the cross—your sin and my sin.

The next time you feel forsaken and lift up your voice to Almighty God, do this: Go to a private place and spend time reflecting on the incredible truth that the One who hears your

The One who hears your prayers has been there too. He knows exactly how you feel. He knows what it means to be forsaken.

prayers has been there too. He knows exactly how you feel. He knows what it means to be forsaken.

And here is the truth you can depend on when you feel forsaken: Jesus hung on the cross, and God turned His back on His Son so that He would never have to turn His back on you. That was the excruciating price He paid because He loves you that much. He loved and died and suffered on this earth so you wouldn't be forsaken.

We Feel Frustrated

Have you felt frustrated with God lately? If we're honest, we've all had times when we've said, or felt like saying, "Lord, I've been praying about this for months, for years, and it doesn't seem as if You've been listening."

Listen to the words of the psalmist in the second verse of Psalm 13: "How long shall I take counsel in my soul, having sorrow in my heart daily? How long will my enemy be exalted over me?"

David was frustrated for two reasons in that moment. First, he was frustrated because of his own emotions. He was basically saying, "Every day I go through this. Every day I have to deal with this."

Someone said the problem with life is that it's so daily. Each morning we rise and face our challenges, and the same ones are there every day, rain or shine, summer, winter, spring, or fall.

Whatever we have to deal with, whenever we get up and "reboot" our minds, the same issues return from the day before.

Have you ever experienced the frustration of something painful or negative becoming your constant and daily companion? Of course, you know what to do in such moments. You've been taught to read your Bible, pray, and spend time with God's people. But you're no longer dealing with a problem; the problem is now dealing with you. And your personal "thorn in the flesh" has taken over, and it has gotten you into such an emotional bind that you feel unable to do the thing you should do.

That is what happened to David. He was frustrated by his emotions.

David was also frustrated because of his enemy. "How long will my enemy be exalted over me?" (v. 2). Remember, David was the king in waiting, and he waited fifteen long years between the moment he was promised the kingdom and the moment he actually received it. Much of that time was spent dealing with Saul, his enemy.

As a result, David was essentially shaking his fist at the sky and asking, "How long, Lord, is my enemy going to be exalted over me? Whose side are You on, God?" God seemed to give Saul everything, and David got nothing.

Aren't you glad the psalm doesn't stop there? David may have thought he didn't have a prayer, but in fact, he was just where God wanted him to be.

OUR SUPPLICATION
WHEN GOD DELAYS

As I mentioned, we know we're supposed to pray during difficult times, including those moments when God delays in answering our prayers. So let's take a closer look at David's petitions in this psalm.

In his desperation, David prayed three prayers in Psalm 13 verse 3. First he said, "Consider me." The words actually mean "Lord, look on me. Look at me." What he wanted to say was, "Lord, don't turn Your back on me anymore. Turn around and see me!"

His second prayer is, "Hear me." David was pleading with God to answer his questions. "Lord, please hear what I'm saying."

And then there's this very curious third request. He said, "Enlighten my eyes." When I first read that prayer, my understanding was that David was asking the Lord to give him the insight he might lack—to "enlighten" his understanding. But that's not the meaning of the phrase. Here's what it means. David was saying, "Lord, put the light back in my eyes." Isn't that a curious thing to put in our prayers? *Put the light back in my eyes.*

You can easily spot a person who is suffering from depression. Their face reveals their state of mind. Depression transforms one's countenance into a mask, empty and rigid. Most of all, the light in the person's eyes is extinguished. That's where David

"O Lord, I have no hope. Please see me, please hear me, and oh God, put the light back in my eyes."

was, and he prayed, "O Lord, I have no hope. Please *see* me, please *hear* me, and oh God, put the light back in my eyes."

What a moving prayer!

Now, notice that David wasn't praying to a vague or generalized version of God. Instead, he used two specific names for God in that single verse: "Consider and hear me. O LORD [Jehovah] my God [Elohim]; enlighten my eyes" (Psalm 13:3).

Jehovah reflects God's promises; *Elohim* reflects God's power. So David was saying, "O God of power and promise, I appeal to You."

In this moment of transformation, I believe David's mind went back to the promise he'd been given—the promise that he would be king. I believe he had a resurgence of faith that he would sit on Israel's throne. God had promised him something, and despite all that had transpired, that meant something to David. His heart suddenly realized and returned to the conviction that the God who promises is the God who is powerful enough to stand behind His promises.

In other words, David's faith rebounded and reasserted itself.

I often think of Jeremiah 20:11 when I'm facing unexpected challenges. Here's what it says: "The LORD is with me as a mighty, awesome One. Therefore my persecutors will stumble, and will not prevail. They will be greatly ashamed, for they will not prosper. Their everlasting confusion will never be forgotten."

There's a similar promise in Psalm 138: "Though I walk in the midst of trouble, You will revive me; You will stretch out Your hand against the wrath of my enemies, and Your right hand will save me. The LORD will perfect that which concerns me; Your mercy, O LORD, endures forever; do not forsake the works of Your hands" (vv. 7–8).

We can find tremendous hope of ultimate victory even in the deepest pits of life. But it's not a simple process. There isn't a handy, guaranteed formula for hope in the midst of suffering. It takes absolute, fall-on-your-face humility and genuine, gut-wrenchingly honest prayer.

We must come to the point where we hear ourselves say, "Lord God, my life is devastated. I've been victimized by my emotions and overwhelmed by my problems. Life has thrown all it can at me, and I've caved in. I've experienced none of the victory; I haven't honored You. I am at the point of surrender. But O Lord God, in the midst of all this, help me to see and know my Mighty Awesome One, *Jehovah Elohim*."

OUR SONG WHEN GOD DELAYS

There is a threefold progression in this psalm, moving from tears to triumph. Right in the center lies the ultimate truth that makes the difference. That truth is that *Jehovah Elohim*—Almighty God—is in charge. No wonder David broke into joyful song!

Notice that David's song is a song of triumph. In Psalm 13 verses 5 and 6 he wrote, "But I have trusted in Your mercy; my heart shall rejoice in Your salvation. I will sing to the LORD, because He has dealt bountifully with me."

How did David reach that point of triumph? He began to see God.

Our troubles can cause us to avoid the places where we're most likely to see God. Have you ever noticed that? I'm always puzzled when troubled people fall away from the church. They may be strong pillars of the local fellowship, but when trouble comes along, they disappear.

Here's the truth: If you are experiencing difficulty, get up early and go to both services! You need all the church you can get when you're in a time of heartache or suffering—a time when God's answers to your prayers have been delayed.

Our faith isn't a luxury intended for periods of smooth sailing. Neither is our fellowship. When trouble comes along, that's when it's wonderful to be part of a faithful, Bible-believing body of people who will rally around you and help you. They'll pray for you and support you with their resources, they'll encourage you, and they'll counsel you. The only one whose opinion you should take a sabbatical from during hard times is the devil—not the Church.

The only one whose opinion you should take a sabbatical from during hard times is the devil—not the Church.

Our song is a song of triumph, and it's also a song of thanksgiving. David wrote in verse 6, "I will sing to the LORD, because He has dealt bountifully with me."

My friend, if you want to stay healthy as a Christian, you need to remember what God has done for you in the past. The devil attempts to minimize everything God has done for you and to maximize all your problems. Don't let him do that. You need to remember God's goodness in the moments when you are feeling alone and disheartened.

I wrote in my Bible one day, "Don't forget to polish your monuments." Meaning, don't forget to polish the monuments of victory in your life. That's the most wonderful reason for keeping a journal. Here, David consulted the journal in his mind regarding his dealings with his Lord, and he realized, "God has dealt bountifully with me."

What a terrible thing it is to become trapped in the confining walls of the present. Sadly, that is often our first impulse. The clear and present danger is so imposing in our mind that it blocks our view behind us so we don't see and remember the Lord's blessings, and obscures the future so we fear what is to come. We desperately need perspective. We have no control over the future, but we can gain wisdom from the past. As we remember who God is and His faithfulness to us in the past, we will then reassert, without hesitation, our confidence in His ability to meet the needs of our present situation as well as our future.

So make your list. What has God done for you? Make a detailed inventory of His faithfulness in your life, and you'll be surprised at what He has done.

Psalm 28:7 says it this way: "The LORD is my strength and my shield; my heart trusted in Him, and I am helped; therefore my heart greatly rejoices, and with my song I will praise Him."

Does it seem strange to you that Psalm 13, so filled with misery, builds to a final note of triumph, trust, and praise to Almighty God? In reality, there is nothing strange about it at all! That's the way faith should work. We come to God and pour out our heart to Him, and we experience renewed faith as He prods our memory and reaffirms His love for us.

The same God who has been there for you in the past is the One who is going to be there for you in the future. He will bring resolution in His own time, according to His own purposes. We often become preoccupied with our circumstances, but God is focused on our character. In His wisdom there is a purpose for His seeming delay, or even when His answer is no. He is working for our greater good; His purposes are beyond our finite understanding.

So keep praying. Keep trusting. Keep reaching out to Him even when it seems He has not heard or answered your prayer. Because the truth is that God has not forgotten you, He has always been faithful to you, and your answer is coming.

Nine

GOD HAS NOT FORGOTTEN
YOU WHEN DREAMS DIE

My home state of California is known for many things: sunshine, lovely scenery, the ocean, incredible natural parks, technological innovation, high taxes, and more. Unfortunately, in recent years, my West Coast home has also gained notoriety for the high number of wildfires occurring in our dry seasons and beyond.

Of course, Californians have been familiar with large fires for decades. In many ways they are a part of life, just like mudslides, earthquakes, and other natural disasters. However, the recent spate of fires have been both numerous and massive—and especially deadly. Millions of acres have been consumed in these blazes, along with hundreds of lives.

When news reporters interview survivors in the aftermath of such fires, one phrase gets repeated over and over: "We lost everything."

One resident gave the following account when wildfires tore through the wine country fifty miles northeast of San Francisco in September 2020:

> The entire side of the hill was on fire—all trees, all burning, all roaring like a jet. . . . At that moment we realized that it was time to go. We [later] found out that our house was indeed gone. It's a very sobering thing to find out that all you've worked for and all that your parents have worked for, in a moment, is gone. It gives you pause. And it gives you a moment to realize what's really important in life. Because what we thought was important is now ashes.[1]

Our hearts break when we hear stories like this. It is wonderful news that this man and his family survived. And his take on what happened reveals the correct perspective: "It gives you a moment to realize what's really important in life."

Still, that perspective was gained at a high cost. A deep loss. When people lose their homes and businesses in such a quick and dramatic fashion, there is more involved than the loss of wood and brick, photos and furniture, paperwork and equipment.

There is the loss of a dream.

Have you dealt with such a loss? Perhaps not the complete loss of your home, but what about the loss of your dream job? What about the loss of your dream marriage, your dream ministry, or your dream retirement?

Such losses are devastating because our dreams are a reflection of who we are—our passions and values, hopes and desires, plans and priorities. How could we become deprived of such dreams and not believe that God has forgotten us?

The key to recovering from deep loss—especially the loss of a dream—is to *let God*. Specifically, here are four steps you can take: Let God comfort you, let God restore you, let God redirect you, and let God use you.

LET GOD COMFORT YOU

First, let God comfort you. In a time of loss, our greatest need is immediate and effective comfort.

When Job suffered the loss of all he had, his three friends came "to comfort him" (Job 2:11). They failed in their task, for they tried to comfort him with "empty words" (21:34). Job finally muttered in disgust, "Miserable comforters are you all!" (16:2). In the end, only God could comfort him by teaching him valuable lessons, deepening his faith, and restoring the things Job had lost.

The psalmist expressed his praise in Psalm 71 for having a God who comforted him "on every side" (v. 21). He said in Psalm 94:19, "In the multitude of my anxieties within me, Your comforts delight my soul." In Psalm 119:50, we read, "This is my comfort in my affliction, for Your word has given me life."

Speaking to exiles and refugees who had lost not only their homes but their very nation, the Lord said in Isaiah 51:12, "I, even I, am He who comforts you."

The Holy Spirit is called the Comforter in John's Gospel. And the apostle Paul described our Lord as the "God of all comfort" and as the One who "comforts the downcast" (2 Corinthians 1:3; 7:6). It's for this reason the Bible tells us to "be of good comfort" (2 Corinthians 13:11).

If you're distressed over something you've lost, this might be a good time to go to the concordance at the back of your Bible (or online) and look up all 106 references in the Bible to the word *comfort*. If out of our loss we discover the reassuring ministry of the God of all comfort, we will gain great treasure.

The reason God is such a comfort in times of loss is because He is the one "thing" we can never lose. The greatest silver lining in the dark cloud of loss is that we are reminded—perhaps even

If out of our loss we discover the reassuring ministry of the God of all comfort, we will gain great treasure.

forced—to remember that God alone will always be with us. He has promised never to leave us or forsake us (Hebrews 13:5).

LET GOD RESTORE YOU

Second, let God restore you. In the book written by the ancient prophet Joel, the Lord told the people who had lost their crops, "I will repay you for the years the locusts have eaten. . . . You will have plenty to eat, until you are full, and you will praise the name of the LORD your God, who has worked wonders for you" (Joel 2:25–26 NIV).

We often find that times of great loss are also times of great lessons learned—if we can only persevere by faith.

William Carey, the father of modern missions, wanted to translate the Bible into as many Indian languages as possible. He established a large print shop in Serampore where translation work was being done. Carey was away from Serampore on March 11, 1812, but his associate, William Ward, was working late. Suddenly Ward's throat tightened, and he smelled smoke. He leaped up to discover clouds belching from the printing room. He screamed for help, and workers passed water from the nearby river until two o'clock in the morning.

It was to no avail. Everything was destroyed.

On March 12, missionary Joshua Marshman entered a Calcutta classroom where Carey was teaching. "I can think of no easy way to break the news," he said. "The print shop burned to the ground last night." Gone were Carey's massive polyglot dictionary, two grammar books, and whole versions of the Bible. Gone were sets of type for 14 eastern languages, 1,200 reams of paper, 55,000 printed sheets, and 30 pages of his Bengal dictionary. Gone was his complete library.

"The work of years—gone in a moment," Carey whispered.

He took little time to mourn. "The loss is heavy," he wrote, "but as traveling a road the second time is usually done with greater ease and certainty than the first time, so I trust the work will lose nothing of real value. We are not discouraged; indeed the work is already begun again in every language. We are cast down but not in despair."

When news of the fire reached England, it catapulted Carey to instant fame. Thousands of pounds were raised for his work, and volunteers offered to help. The enterprise was rebuilt and enlarged. By 1832, complete Bibles, New Testaments, or separate books of Scripture had been issued from the printing press in forty-four languages and dialects.

The secret of Carey's success is found in his resiliency. "There are grave difficulties on every hand," he once wrote, "and more are looming ahead. Therefore we must go forward."[2]

"We are cast down

but not in despair."

The same is true when we suffer loss—even the loss of our dreams. There is no room for self-pity in the heart of God's children. No room for bitterness or rage. When a dream is lost, we must make the choice to continue forward and serve our King in whichever direction He leads.

Yet how do we determine that direction?

LET GOD REDIRECT YOU

There is an interesting story in the Gospel of Luke about Jesus healing a man possessed by many demons—so many they called themselves "Legion." This man was known throughout his community because the demons drove him to extreme behavior. "He wore no clothes," wrote Luke, "nor did he live in a house but in the tombs" (Luke 8:27). Also, "he was kept under guard, bound with chains and shackles; and he broke the bonds and was driven by the demon into the wilderness" (v. 29).

This man experienced a miraculous healing when he encountered Jesus. The Son of God rebuked the demons and commanded them to leave the man, but He did allow them to inhabit a herd of pigs that was nearby. Immediately, the pigs rushed into the sea and drowned.

As you might expect, this man desired to follow Jesus after

such an incredible healing. He wanted to become one of Jesus' disciples and travel with Him.

What you might not expect, however, is Jesus' response: "Now the man from whom the demons had departed begged Him that he might be with Him. But Jesus sent him away, saying, 'Return to your own house, and tell what great things God has done for you.' And he went his way and proclaimed throughout the whole city what great things Jesus had done for him" (vv. 38–39).

In many ways, this man had a dream—a short-lived dream, yes, but still an intense desire. He had encountered the One who had the power to free him from his demons. He wanted nothing more than to become a follower of Jesus.

Knowing the Gospels, we would expect Jesus to embrace such a dream. After all, this is the same Savior who called people from all manner of backgrounds and circumstances to join Him, learn from Him, and become contributors in His kingdom. This is the same Messiah who said, "Pray the Lord of the harvest to send out laborers into His harvest" (Matthew 9:38).

So why did Jesus reject this man? Why did Jesus refuse his offer to become a disciple?

The answer is that Jesus did not *reject* the former demoniac; He *redirected* him. The man wanted to follow Christ by traveling with Him, but Christ had a different plan: "Return to your

Jesus did not reject the former demoniac, He redirected him.

own house, and tell what great things God has done for you." In short, Jesus turned this man into an evangelist rather than an apprentice.

Here's a truth that we may not like, but it is still a truth nonetheless: Sometimes our dreams die because they were not the right dreams—they weren't the dreams God has for us. Sometimes God closes the door on our deepest desires and brightest hopes.

When that happens, it's our job to let those dreams go and instead embrace whatever new direction God has for us. Because our ultimate goal is not to fulfill *our* ultimate dream but to be useful in God's kingdom.

LET GOD USE YOU

Finally, in times of loss, we enter an opportunity in which we can become more helpful to other people. The book of 2 Corinthians, in which Paul described the hardships of his work, opens with these words: "Blessed be the God and Father of our Lord Jesus Christ, the Father of mercies and God of all comfort, who comforts us in all our tribulation, that we may be able to comfort those who are in any trouble, with the comfort with which we ourselves are comforted by God" (2 Corinthians 1:2–4).

Richard Wurmbrand is a good example of someone who

suffered hardship in his work. In his book *Tortured for Christ*, he tells of being in and out of Communist prisons due to persecution. Despite the loss of possessions and freedom, the principle of tithing was so internalized in his heart and in those of his fellow prisoners that when they received a slice of bread a week and dirty soup every day, they faithfully tithed from it. Every tenth week they took their slice of bread and gave it to fellow prisoners in Jesus' name.[3]

Wurmbrand understood the value of being used by God.

So should we.

When disaster strikes, we may grieve over the loss of things once held dear, and especially over the loss of dreams we hoped to achieve. That's natural. But upon deeper, prayerful reflection, we eventually come to realize we can't take any of these things with us to heaven; all will perish in the final conflagration.

But the God of comfort strengthens our heart, provides for our needs, and uses us for His glory. Knowing this, we can strengthen ourselves in His peace, His provision, His presence, and His promises.

He is the God of all comfort, and He will never forget His plans and dreams for your life.

WHAT TO DO WHEN YOU
FEEL FORGOTTEN

It was a story that gripped the world for weeks. On June 23, 2018, a youth soccer coach led the twelve members of his team into a system of caves in the Chiang Rai province of Thailand. He viewed it as a team-building exercise. A fun excursion.

Unfortunately, a storm unleashed monsoon levels of rainwater into the cave system while the boys spent an hour exploring inside. When the coach tried to lead them out, he found much of the caves had been flooded. They were impassable, though the coach tried several times to swim for a way out.

Soon the realization hit with the force of a blow: The coach and his young team were trapped.

Fortunately, several of the boys had left their bicycles outside the mouth of the caves. When some of the boys' parents contacted local officials to report their missing sons, park officials found the bikes and were able to determine what had happened.

Even so, the cave system is several miles long, and torrential rains continued to fill the tunnels with water. Rescuers had little idea where to look for the soccer team, nor did they have any confirmation that the coach and the boys were still alive. Had they been drowned in the flood? If they were alive, would they have access to oxygen long enough for a rescue attempt? Did they have food of any kind?

It took nine days for rescuers to make contact with the children and their coach. Nine days! Incredibly, all of them were still alive, although many were in bad shape. Workers were able to provide food and additional oxygen, but the rescue was still a difficult task—largely because most of the children didn't know how to swim.

In the end, it took an additional eight days to prepare for and execute the rescue attempt. The children were brought through the network of caves one at a time accompanied by professional divers from the Thai equivalent of the Navy SEALs. All twelve of the boys survived, as did their coach.

They had gone into the cave with a single flashlight, a few

batteries, and a few snacks to last the afternoon. All told, they spent seventeen long days in those caves.[1]

Can you imagine those first nine days? Because of the rising water, the coach led his charges up onto a ledge, where they were forced to crowd together as they hoped for rescue. But what hope did they have?

Imagine what it must have felt like on that ledge surrounded by darkness and a depth of silence none of them had ever experienced. None of the familiar sounds of their city—no cars driving along the roads, no delivery trucks honking, no occasional airplanes flying overhead. They didn't hear their parents' voices. They didn't hear their favorite songs or television shows. They didn't hear the laughter or chatter of their school friends. They heard no sounds at all except the dripping of water and the occasional sob of a teammate.

The boys had no way of knowing whether anyone was looking for them. As the days continued to tick by, they must have felt completely forgotten.

REMEMBER GOD'S REALITY

Of course, the reality is that nothing could have been further from the truth. The boys in that cave were far from forgotten!

For days, news of their plight captured the hearts and imaginations of people all around the globe. They were the lead story not only on local news stations in Thailand but on every news station in just about every country. World leaders were paying attention, including the president of the United States and heads of state throughout Europe. Resources had been diverted and rushed to the boys' aid. Celebrities from John Legend to Elon Musk raised awareness and offered help.

And when the news broke that the boys had been discovered alive on that ninth day, the entire world erupted with joy.

There's a lesson for us in their story if we're willing to see it. The boys felt isolated and completely alone in that dark cave; it seemed as if nobody was even aware of their plight. In reality, more people than they could have imagined were pulling for them and praying for them and pushing through obstacle after obstacle to rescue them.

What can we do when we feel like God has forgotten about us? First of all, we can remember the reality of who God is and what He has done. In order to accomplish that, it may be necessary to differentiate between *feelings* and *truth*.

Now, I don't want to give the impression that feelings are unimportant. They are not. Nor am I implying that feelings are not real. They are very much real, which is why they can affect us so deeply.

What I am saying is that there can be a disconnect between our feelings and the reality of our situation.

For example, as we have seen throughout this book, it's common for people to feel as if God has forgotten them. You and I have felt that way at times, and we may possibly feel that way in the future. It's part of life. Not only that, the men and women chronicled in God's Word felt that way—Moses, David, Jeremiah, Hannah, Job, the apostles, and more. Even Jesus cried out on the cross, "My God, My God, why have You forsaken Me?" (Matthew 27:46).

Those feelings are real. They matter. They influence not only our thoughts but also our actions. And they can cause us real and lasting pain *if* we allow them to take hold of us.

Yet those feelings don't reflect reality. That's because God cannot forget us. It's impossible for Him to do so given His nature—given who He is. God knows all things, and as we've seen for nine chapters now, God takes special care to actively monitor us and guide us through every moment of our lives.

The reality is that you are *never* forgotten. Not by God.

Here are some practical steps you can take when your feelings come into conflict with that reality.

- *Identify your feelings.* One of the most difficult aspects about separating our feelings from reality is how our thinking is

God cannot forget us. It's
impossible for Him to do so given
His nature—given who He is.

often affected by those same feelings. So, one of the first things we can do when it seems like God has forgotten about us is to identify what we are feeling. Ask yourself, *What am I feeling, specifically? Am I angry? Frustrated? Lonely? Grieving? Exhausted? Anxious? Bitter? Bored?*

- *Express your feelings to God.* Once you identify your feelings and recognize how they are affecting your emotions, turn them over to God through prayer. Speak with Him about your feelings. Be specific, and don't hold back. Be completely honest. Getting those feelings off your chest is an important step toward emotional and spiritual healing by giving your cares to God. "Cast your burden on the Lord, and He shall sustain you" (Psalm 55:22).

- *Express your feelings to others.* Talking with others about your feelings is another helpful step when it seems as if God has forgotten you. Of course, I recommend speaking with people you know and trust—people who know the Word of God and are spiritually mature. Be open about your feelings, and then give your counselor the opportunity to offer guidance and care from the Word of God. As Scripture says, "Bear one another's burdens, and so fulfill the law of Christ" (Galatians 6:2).

- *Identify what you know to be true.* Negative feelings often overwhelm us based on something we "think" is true or something that "might" be true—such as the idea that God doesn't care. Such speculations are unhelpful. What is helpful is identifying what you *know* to be true about whatever situation is causing you to feel abandoned. For instance, *What do I know to be true of God's character? What are the facts in my current circumstance?*

- *Express what is true to both God and others.* Being aware of what is true is important, but talking through that reality in prayer or in conversation with others is key to separating feelings from reality. Make the effort to verbally express what is true and it will cement that truth in your mind and heart.

REFLECT GOD'S LIGHT

During news coverage of the crisis in Thailand, I remember how much emphasis the reporters placed on the boys' lack of food, shelter, blankets, and other supplies. And of course they were right to be concerned about those needs—the soccer team and its coach were in desperate straits.

However, I found myself focusing on another tragic aspect of their situation: the lack of light.

If you have ever been in a cave of any size, you have probably turned off your flashlight at some point just to see what would happen. It's hard to imagine what impenetrable darkness feels like until you experience it. There are no words to describe the sensation of opening your eyes as wide as possible, placing your hand directly in front of your face—and seeing nothing. Yet those boys in that cave endured that reality for nine whole days. Nothing but darkness. The complete absence of light.

In our lives, there are times when we feel surrounded by emotional or spiritual darkness. Circumstances can become so bleak that we feel shrouded by them—which is a major reason we often feel forgotten. When we can't "see" God or trace His hand because of the events in our lives, it's easy to believe He no longer cares.

For these reasons and more, I want to offer two truths you need to remember during those seasons of darkness.

Jesus Is the Light of the World

Jesus was teaching in the temple one day when He was interrupted in an unusual way: "Then the scribes and Pharisees brought to Him a woman caught in adultery. And when they had set her in the midst, they said to Him, 'Teacher, this woman was caught in adultery, in the very act. Now Moses, in the law, commanded us that such should be stoned. But what do You say?'" (John 8:3–5).

First of all, can you imagine someone pulling such a stunt

today? Can you imagine a pastor delivering a message on Sunday morning and then several elders from the church bursting through the doors and making these kinds of accusations in front of everyone?

The actions of the Pharisees and other religious leaders revealed how desperate they were to stop Jesus' momentum and regain their previous levels of authority and respect. In this moment, they thought they had trapped Jesus between a rock and a hard place. Only the Roman authorities could put someone to death at that time in Jerusalem, so they could have Jesus arrested if He attempted to enforce Moses' law by suggesting the woman be stoned. But if Jesus recommended disobeying the laws of their people, they thought He would lose the respect of the crowd.

You are likely familiar with the rest of the story. Jesus took some time to draw in the sand, allowing the tension to build as the Pharisees continued to pepper Him with questions. Then He dropped the hammer on those seeking to shame Him: "He who is without sin among you, let him throw a stone at her first" (v. 7).

Stung by their own hypocrisy, the instigators left. Turning to the woman, Jesus said to her, "Neither do I condemn you; go and sin no more" (v. 11). The story serves as a familiar and much-loved demonstration of God's grace.

Yet look at what happened afterward. The very next verse

says that Jesus turned back to the crowd and resumed His teaching by offering this truth: "I am the light of the world. He who follows Me shall not walk in darkness, but have the light of life" (v. 12).

I cannot imagine how dark that moment must have been for the woman Jesus rescued. She had made the choice to sin, yes, but then she was accosted by strangers and dragged out into public view, likely with no clothes to shield her. (Notice the man was not dragged away with her.) Then she was thrown down in front of everyone at the temple and threatened with stoning—a truly terrible form of capital punishment. And then, draped in her shame and humiliation, she was forced to look into the eyes of Christ.

She found kindness in those eyes. Forgiveness. Grace. And in that moment, the darkness was banished.

Jesus, the Light of the world, broke through and offered her hope.

He does the same for you and me. Yes, times of darkness will come. We will endure seasons when it *seems* as if nothing is going right and we are oppressed on every side. Yet if we draw close to Christ in those moments, we will experience His light.

How can we make that happen? Here are some practical ways to seek out Christ and increase your trust in Him even when the darkness feels impenetrable.

- *Memorize verses from God's Word.* If there's one thing I've learned from all my decades of ministry, it's that the Bible is no ordinary book. The Bible is alive—"Living and powerful," as it says in Hebrews 4:12. God's Word has a critical role to play in our lives, but it's up to us to expose ourselves and submit ourselves to that Word. The best way to accomplish this is to memorize Scripture; specifically, we can memorize verses that offer a direct solution to our areas of need. For example, here are some specific Scripture passages to memorize so you'll have access to them whenever it seems as if God has forgotten about you:

> Can a woman forget her nursing child,
> And not have compassion on the son of her womb?
> Surely they may forget,
> Yet I will not forget you. (Isaiah 49:15)

> My God shall supply all your need according to His riches in glory by Christ Jesus. (Philippians 4:19)

> Be strong and of good courage, do not fear nor be afraid of them; for the LORD your God, He is the One who goes with you. He will not leave you nor forsake you. (Deuteronomy 31:6)

Cast your burden on the LORD,

And He shall sustain you;

He shall never permit the righteous to be moved.

(Psalm 55:22)

- *Write out verses from God's Word.* Memorization is a critical discipline for followers of Christ, but it's also helpful to display God's Word so we see it regularly. One way to accomplish this is to handwrite Scripture verses that have a special application for your life in your current season, and then display those verses in places where they will be seen throughout your day—your bathroom mirror, your car, your kitchen table, the frame around your front door, and so on.
- *Keep a prayer journal.* When you're in a spiritually dark season, nothing lets in the Light better than reviewing the many ways God has been faithful to you in the past. However, that's difficult to do if you don't have a record of His faithfulness. So I highly recommend that followers of Christ keep a record of their prayers. Simply record what you are praying about each day. Then, when God answers your prayers, record the answer as well. This will give you a tangible record of God's ongoing light in your life.

You Are the Light of the World

The Sermon on the Mount is the most famous and best-loved sermon ever preached. Recorded in Matthew 5–7, Jesus' teachings in that moment have resonated for centuries as a primary and foundational expression of the Christian life.

One element of those teachings might sound interesting, even strange, given what we just read in the pages above:

> You are the light of the world. A city that is set on a hill cannot be hidden. Nor do they light a lamp and put it under a basket, but on a lampstand, and it gives light to all who are in the house. Let your light so shine before men, that they may see your good works and glorify your Father in heaven. (Matthew 5:14–16)

Jesus was very specific in His language: "*You* are the light of the world." Yet how can we align that sentiment with what we already encountered from John 8:12? In that verse Jesus said, "*I* am the light of the world."

Which is it? Is Jesus the Light of the world, or is it us?

The answer, of course, is both. Jesus is the Light of the world, but His followers have been imbued and filled with His Holy Spirit. Therefore, Christians both reflect Jesus' light *and* serve as lanterns through which God shines His light.

Don't miss the second section of Jesus' teaching: "Let your light so shine before men, that they may see your good works and glorify your Father in heaven." When we are facing a season of darkness—when it seems like even God has forgotten about us—it's easy to become fixated on ourselves. It's easy to think only of ourselves.

However, followers of Jesus are called to live with an external focus. We are tasked with shining God's light into the darkness of our world and ministering to the people around us who are walking through dark times and feeling abandoned. We have a huge role to play in helping others recognize that God is at work in the world—that He has not forgotten them—and He has a plan of redemption that will assure them of a home in heaven one day.

That's the wonderful thing about living for Christ. The more we give of ourselves, the more we gain. The more we invest our resources into God's kingdom—our time, treasure, and talents—the greater the harvest both for today and for eternity. And as we actively choose to model Jesus in our daily lives, our own issues and trials will fade in importance. Having Jesus with us on our life journey, we are reminded of God's unconditional love for us, that He has a purpose for our pain and a plan to use us for His glory. We can trust our lives into His loving care.

For those reasons and more, here are several practical steps you can take to serve as the light of the world whenever you feel the darkness encroaching.

- *Invest your time in others.* Every church that has ever existed has needed volunteers to run and serve in its various ministries. Your church is no exception. There are many opportunities right now for you to make that investment and be a blessing in the lives of others. Choose an outreach that matches your time and talents, and do it with an expectant heart.
- *Invest your money in others.* Yes, it is important to support your local church through your regular tithes and offerings. That is God's plan for the church. But we do not need to stop there—you can also make a difference in other ways. Here is a challenge: At the beginning of the day, take a specific amount of money in cash—even if you can afford only a small amount—and place it in your purse or wallet. Then pray, *Lord God, this is Your money, and I want to be a vessel of Your light to someone today. Please grant me an opportunity to use this money in a way that will bless others in Your name.* After praying, watch for a God-given opportunity to bless someone. Then do it!
- *Follow Jesus' instructions for bringing light to the world.* God has not left everything to our own imaginations

when it comes to serving others. Instead, many passages of Scripture offer specific instructions and commands for loving our neighbor as ourselves. Here is an important one from Jesus Himself:

> The righteous will answer Him, saying, "Lord, when did we see You hungry and feed You, or thirsty and give You drink? When did we see You a stranger and take You in, or naked and clothe You? Or when did we see You sick, or in prison, and come to You?" And the King will answer and say to them, "Assuredly, I say to you, inasmuch as you did it to one of the least of these My brethren, you did it to Me." (Matthew 25:37–40)

Do you see opportunities in your community to feed the hungry? Find those who are thirsty—whether for water, knowledge, or any other need—and give them a drink. Offer clothes and other resources to those who have little. Help care for the sick. Visit those in prison.

When you do what Jesus asked His followers to do, you will shine His light not only to the world but within your own soul.

Conclusion

NEVER FORGOTTEN

We began this book by discussing David's experiences in a cave, feeling as if God had forgotten about him and forgotten His promises. It's fitting that we end these pages with a similar story.

Psalms 57 and 142 were both written while David hid from his enemy, Saul, within one or more caves in the wilderness surrounding Jerusalem. In both psalms, David poured out his heart to God with words of anguish—which is understandable coming from one who was having a hard time coming to terms with what he was going through.

Yet David also wrote these words in those same dark caves:

> My heart is steadfast, O God, my heart is steadfast;
> I will sing and give praise.
> Awake, my glory!

Awake, lute and harp!
I will awaken the dawn.
I will praise You, O Lord, among the peoples;
I will sing to You among the nations.
For Your mercy reaches unto the heavens,
And Your truth unto the clouds.
Be exalted, O God, above the heavens;
Let Your glory be above all the earth.
(Psalm 57:7–11)

Even in the deep recesses of a cave, David knew he was not forgotten. He knew he could "cry out to the LORD with [his] voice" and "pour out [his] complaint before Him" because he knew that God "knew [his] path" (Psalm 142:1–3). Even if he couldn't see his own hand in front of his face because of the darkness that surrounded him, David knew that God could see him and hear him and would meet him right where he was.

God acts in our darkness according to the words of James 1:5: "If any of you lacks wisdom [If any of you don't know what to do; if you think you've been forgotten], let him ask of God, who gives to all liberally and without reproach, and it will be given to him."

"Without reproach" means God doesn't mind if we ask Him for help. He doesn't criticize or disapprove; He isn't disappointed in us if we need His help. He sees us; He has not forgotten us; He is ready to give to us the help we need.

No matter where you are or what you've experienced in the past, I hope you've learned that God *is* with you. You can live with absolute certainty that God has not forgotten you.

As you live each day secure in that knowledge, shine the light of His goodness into a world that needs His love and presence now more than ever.

NOTES

Introduction
1. J. I. Packer, *Knowing God* (Downers Grove, IL: InterVarsity Press, 1973), 97.
2. Packer, *Knowing God*, 98.
3. Edward Hopper, "Jesus, Savior, Pilot Me," 1871.

Chapter 1: You Are Not Forgotten
1. James Ball, "Costeja González and a Memorable Fight for the 'Right to Be Forgotten'," *Guardian*, May 14, 2014, https://www.theguardian.com/world /blog/2014/may/14/mario-costeja-gonzalez-fight-right-forgotten.
2. Dr. Martyn Lloyd-Jones, *Spiritual Depression: Its Causes and Cures* (London: HarperCollins, 1998).
3. "U.S.S. Theodore Roosevelt," WSFA12 News, September 19, 2001, https://www .wsfa.com/story/477688/uss-theodore-roosevelt/.

Chapter 2: God Has Not Forgotten You
When Life Seems Uncertain
1. Joe Iovino, "Shaped by Tragedy and Grace: Wesley's Rescue from Fire," United Methodist Church, February 7, 2017, https://www.umc.org/en /content/shaped-by-tragedy-and-grace-wesleys-rescue-from-fire.
2. Iovino, "Shaped by Tragedy and Grace."

Chapter 3: God Has Not Forgotten
You When You Feel Anxious

1. Todd Archer, "Cowboys' Prescott Got Help for Anxiety, Depression During Offseason," ESPN.com, September 10, 2020, https://www .espn.com/nfl/story/_/id/29854487/cowboys-prescott-got-help-anxiety -depression-offseason.
2. "Managing Stress and Anxiety," Anxiety and Depression Association of America, https://adaa.org/living-with-anxiety/managing-anxiety.
3. "Causes of Anxiety," WebMD, September 12, 2020, https://www .webmd.com/anxiety-panic/guide/causes-anxiety.
4. Erastus Johnson, "The Rock That Is Higher than I," 1871.

Chapter 4: God Has Not Forgotten You When Times Change

1. Robert J. Morgan, *The Red Sea Rules* (Nashville, TN: Thomas Nelson, 2001).
2. Charles Henry Mackintosh, *Notes on the Pentateuch, Volume 2: Exodus* (London: Morrish, 1858), 172.
3. Robert J. Morgan, *The Red Sea Rules* (Nashville, TN: Thomas Nelson, 2001).

Chapter 5: God Has Not Forgotten You
When Your Family Is Hurting

1. The quotes and insights from Dr. Earl McQuay come from his book *Beyond Eagles: A Father's Grief and Hope* (Columbus, GA: Grill Publications, 1987).
2. McQuay, *Beyond Eagles*.

Chapter 6: God Has Not Forgotten You When You Are Lonely

1. *Inspired Faith: 365 Days a Year* (Nashville, TN: Thomas Nelson, 2012), 205.

2. Vance Havner, *Though I Walk Through the Valley* (Old Tappen, NJ: Fleming H. Revell Co., 1974), 71.

3. Christina Tsai, *Queen of the Dark Chamber* (Chicago: Moody Publishers, 1953).

Chapter 7: God Has Not Forgotten You When Health Fails

1. Daniel Jameson and Ali Wunderman, "The Most Dangerous Animals in the World," *Conde Nast Traveler*, November 25, 2020.

2. Methodius, "Are Thy Toils and Woes Increasing," trans. John Mason Neale (1862).

3. Quoted by Robert J. Morgan, *The Promise: God Works All Things Together for Your Good* (Nashville, TN: B&H Publishing Group, 2010), 90.

4. Robert J. Morgan, *From This Verse* (Nashville, TN: Thomas Nelson, 1998), entry for August 13.

Chapter 8: God Has Not Forgotten You When Prayers Go Unanswered

1. Transcript, "Canada Post Delivered This Man's Hair Cream 8 Years After He Ordered It," *As It Happens*, May 26, 2020, https://www.cbc.ca/radio/asithappens/as-it-happens-monday-edition-1.5583557/canada-post-delivered-this-man-s-hair-cream-8-years-after-he-ordered-it-1.5585434.

Chapter 9: God Has Not Forgotten You When Dreams Die

1. "California Wildfire Evacuee: 'We Lost Everything,'" *Yahoo! News*, September 29, 2020, https://news.yahoo.com/california-wildfire-evacuee-lost-everything-005949007.html.

2. Robert J. Morgan, *On This Day* (Nashville, TN: Thomas Nelson, 1997), entry for March 12.

3. Richard Wurmbrand, *Tortured for Christ* (Colorado Springs, CO: David C. Cook, 2017).

Chapter 10: What to Do When You Feel Forgotten

1. Pat Ralph and James Pasley, "This Timeline Shows Exactly How the Thai Cave Rescue Unfolded and What's Happened Since," *Business Insider*, June 24, 2019, https://www.businessinsider.com/thai-cave -rescue-timeline-how-it-unfolded-2018-7.

ABOUT THE AUTHOR

Dr. David Jeremiah serves as senior pastor of Shadow Mountain Community Church in El Cajon, California. He is the founder and host of Turning Point, a ministry committed to providing Christians with sound Bible teaching relevant to today's changing times through radio and television, the internet, live events, and resource materials and books. A bestselling author, Dr. Jeremiah has written more than fifty books, including *Agents of Babylon*, *Agents of the Apocalypse*, *Captured by Grace*, *Living with Confidence in a Chaotic World*, *What in the World Is Going On?*, *The Coming Economic Armageddon*, *God Loves You: He Always Has—He Always Will*, and *What Are You Afraid Of?* Dr. Jeremiah's commitment to teaching the complete Word of God continues to make him a sought-after speaker and writer. His passion for reaching the lost and encouraging believers in their faith is demonstrated through his faithful communication of biblical truths. A dedicated family man, Dr. Jeremiah and his wife, Donna, have four grown children and twelve grandchildren. Connect with Dr. Jeremiah on Facebook (@drdavidjeremiah), Twitter (@davidjeremiah), and his website (davidjeremiah.org).

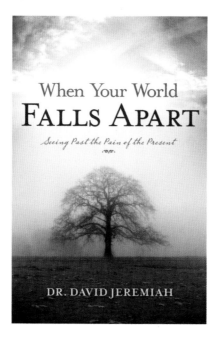

When life suddenly turns upside down, there, in the midst of your trials and in the center of your pain, is God—comforting, guiding, encouraging, teaching, sustaining. In this perceptive and deeply personal book, Dr. David Jeremiah draws from the beautiful poetry and deep truths of the Psalms—passages that gave him comfort and strength on his journey into the unknown. Interwoven with his own reflections and insights are the inspiring real-life stories of other men and women who have faced unexpected adversity and found that God's grace is truly sufficient for every need.

DAVID JEREMIAH

31 DAYS TO
HAPPINESS

Searching for
Heaven on Earth

"Am I happy?" is life's most persistent question—and God's answer, for God's people, is "I want you to be happy." Christians should be the happiest people on earth! But are you? If not, why not? In *31 Days to Happiness*, history's most successful man, Solomon, takes us on his questioning journey into the deeper questions of life in the book of Ecclesiastes. Solomon explores the questions: What was it that pushed you and me into the wrong pursuits? The unwise relationships? The destructive habits? How can we climb out of it now, or is it too late? Through the study and application of the treasures in this book, we can learn much about the school of life as we listen to the voice and wisdom of Solomon. Prepare for age-old secrets to renew and re-create in your heart, mind, body, and spirit the joy you have lost. God longs to bless your life with wisdom and bring you to the crest of a hill where you can catch a glimpse of what seems impossible: heaven on earth.

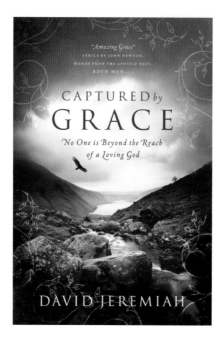

Is there anything you can do that is so bad you can't be forgiven? Can any of your thoughts or actions put you beyond the reach of God's love? In this important study on the topic of grace, David Jeremiah helps you discover that the grace of God is available to you no matter who you are or what you've done. In this compelling book, Dr. Jeremiah uses the beloved hymn "Amazing Grace" and takes the reader on an unforgettable journey as he parallels the life of the songwriter John Newton and the life of the apostle Paul before his conversion. Both were confirmed and proclaimed wretches before the grace of God reached them, but God's grace transformed their lives completely. That same grace is available to all who will receive it.